ELVIS

ELV

The Films and Career of Elvis Presley
by Steven Zmijewsky and Boris Zmijewsky

Citadel Press
Secaucus, New Jersey

Published by Citadel Press
A division of Lyle Stuart, Inc.
120 Enterprise Ave.,
    Secaucus, N. J. 07094
In Canada: George J. McLeod Limited
73 Bathurst St., Toronto, Ont.

Manufactured in the
United States of America

Designed by Peretz Kaminsky

ISBN 0-8065-0511-7

Contents

Acknowledgments

Photos

Courtesy of 20th Century-Fox Corporation, Paramount Pictures Corporation, Metro-Goldwyn-Mayer Studios, United Artists, Allied Artists, National General Corporation. United Press International, National Broadcasting Company, Mark Ricci of *Memory Shop,* Bill Kenly, Lou Valentino, and the authors' private collection.

Biographical sources are the dozens of pressbooks, magazine and newspaper articles (1965–1974) in the extensive microfilm and clippings files of the Lincoln Center Library for Theatre, Jerry Hopkins' informative biography *Elvis,* and Roger Tomlinson's illustrated biography, *Elvis Presley;* and the recollections of numerous Elvis Presley fans who lived through the fifties.

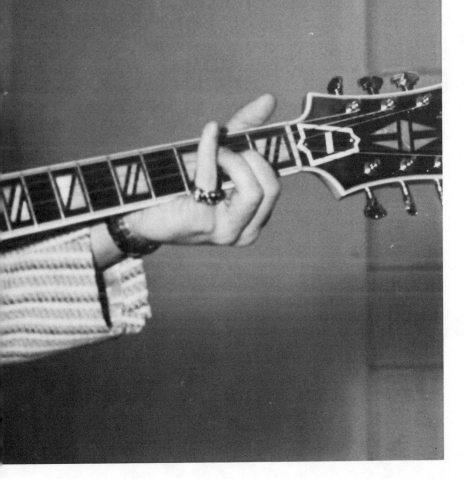

In the Beginning...

Shortly after noon on January 8, 1935, twin sons were born to a teenage sewing-machine operator named Gladys Smith Presley, wife of farm worker Vernon Elvis Presley. The mirror-image twins were named Elvis Aron and Jesse Garon. Jesse Garon died within six hours and was buried the next day in an unmarked grave in the Priceville Cemetery, Tupelo, Mississippi. The other twin, Elvis Aron, lived for some twenty years in relative obscurity and poverty before becoming the single biggest attraction in the history of popular music. And in the following twenty years he became the country's most enduring and successful show business personality. His first name became better known than any two names in the world. He sold over 300 million records, starred in thirty-three films, earned hundreds of millions of dollars, and became the idol of a generation of adolescents all over the world. For he was and is *Elvis Presley*—King of Rock 'n' Roll. In January of 1972, he gave a live concert that was televised via satellite to *500 million* viewers all over the world.

Elvis didn't begin life as a superstar, but as a not particularly handsome child of dirt-poor sharecroppers. There was no indication of anything extraordinary or exceptional in the child's face.

He had huge intelligent eyes, a seemingly flattened nose, drooping lips, and looked round and soft. As an only child he was as spoiled as the

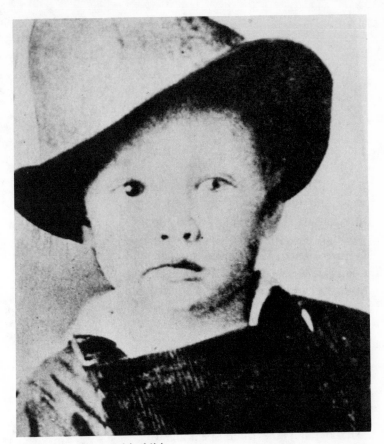

Elvis as two-year-old child

Elvis as teenager

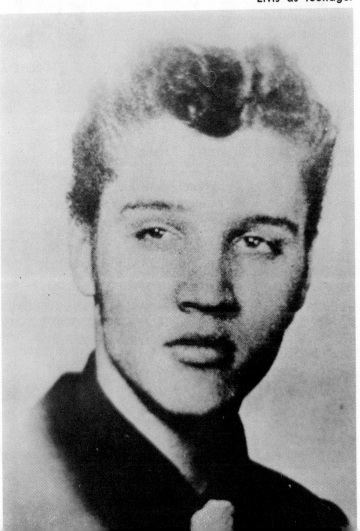

meager family budget could afford. As Elvis remembered: "I never felt poor. There was always shoes to wear and food to eat—yet, I knew there were things my parents did without just to make sure I was clothed and fed." His mother, Gladys, thought he was the greatest thing ever to happen and treated him accordingly from the day he was born to the day she died.

The Presleys were poor, God-fearing folk that taught the young Elvis good manners and a strict brand of Christianity. He was always polite and well-mannered, never failing to add "sir" or "ma'am" when speaking to his elders, never interrupting or arguing, always standing up when elders entered a room. At the zenith of his popularity, even his worst critics said Elvis was, if nothing else, polite. His "Southern manners" were always a sharp contrast to his public image of unrepressed sexuality and near-pagan arrogance on stage.

Elvis's first introduction to music came from church gospel singing. His mother once told the story of Elvis sliding off her lap, running down the aisle of the First Assembly of God Church, and scrambling up to the platform. He would stand looking up at the choir and try to sing along. But he was too little to know the words; he could only carry the tune.

Years later, when asked where he got his wiggle, which sent hordes of teenage girls into near-orgiastic fits, Elvis responded: "We used to go to these religious singin's all the time. There were these singers, perfectly fine singers, but nobody responded to them. Then there was the preacher and they cut up all over the place,

Elvis in ROTC at Humes High School, age 16

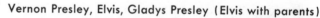

Vernon Presley, Elvis, Gladys Presley (Elvis with parents)

jumpin' on the piano, movin' ever' which way. The audience liked 'em. I guess I learned from them."

Elvis grew up with hardly any friends outside his family. No one associated with the school system in Tupelo remembered much about Elvis before he was in the fifth grade. One day in class he sang the song "Old Shep" so sweetly that the principal of the school carried Elvis to the Mississippi-Alabama Fair and entered him in the annual contest.

Elvis sang "Old Shep" at the fair, standing on a chair and reaching for the microphone, unaccompanied because the guitar players present were reluctant to give help to any of the competition. Elvis won second prize—five dollars and free admission to all the amusement rides.

As Elvis was growing up, his father moved from job to job; from delivering milk to working crops in the bottomlands, sorting lumber and hiring out as an apprentice carpenter in Tupelo. Whatever job he could get he took.

For his twelfth birthday, Elvis was given a guitar instead of the expensive bicycle he wanted. In a few months he taught himself to play a few chords and began listening to the radio, trying to imitate the sounds he heard. He listened to the popular vocalists of the day such as Roy Acuff, Ernest Tubb and Jimmie Rodgers.

In 1948, when Elvis was thirteen years old, the family left Tupelo, hoping to find better prospects elsewhere.

"We were broke, man, broke, and we left Tupelo overnight," recalled

Elvis, "Dad packed all our belongings in boxes and put them on the top and in the trunk of a 1939 Plymouth. We just headed for Memphis."

Things weren't any better in Memphis. At first the family packed themselves into one room of a large box-like home. There were no kitchen facilities and the Presleys shared a bath with three other families. The Presleys slept, cooked and ate all in one room. And initially Elvis had no friends. Largely this was due to his shyness and the fact that a new boy in any neighborhood undergoes a period of painful adaptation. He attended the L.C. Humes High School, which had 1,600 students, more pupils than there were people in East Tupelo.

His father worked for a tool company and drove a truck for a wholesale grocer; his mother sometimes worked in a curtain factory or as a waitress in a downtown cafeteria. The combined Presley income came to about thirty-five dollars a week.

Even with Elvis in high school, his parents continued their coddling and worrying more than the average parent would about their only son. Elvis, in a mild sort of rebellion, began to assume his personality through a very individual style of personal appearance. He wore his hair long and greased, sported long sideburns at a time when every youth in school wore a crew-cut. His clothing was flashy and loud, mostly pink and black. Anywhere he went he stood out like the proverbial sore thumb.

Elvis at 11 years

Elvis at 13 years

Elvis and Priscilla Presley

Elvis was popular with girls, dating regularly and attending parties where he'd sometimes sing and play his guitar. He wasn't an outstanding student, but loved to play football, even though he was too small to play on the school team.

In November of 1950, Elvis was working as an usher at the Loew's State Theatre downtown, from five to ten each night, for $12.75 a week. This gave him a chance to see movies for free, earn a little extra money, and dream of being a movie star. He soon had to quit the job when he began to fall behind in his studies.

In the Humes High yearbook for 1953, there is only one picture of Elvis. He was *not* voted the most outstanding, most popular, most talented, most charming, or most likely to succeed. He was not voted most anything. No one, save his mother, even thought that the pleasant, sensitive, fairly good-looking youth would amount to anything special. True, he played the guitar a little, sang pleasantly enough at parties, but so did many other youngsters in the South.

Elvis graduated from Humes High School in June 1953 and went to work driving a truck for an electric company. He was almost not hired because of his long hair, a rarity in those days. Only shiftless characters and suspicious criminal types wore their hair long, according to the popular consensus of the day.

One day, driving his truck through the streets of Memphis, Elvis noticed the Memphis Recording Service—Make Your Own Records, Four Dollars for Two Songs. He thought that would be a nice birthday present for his mother, a personal record. She always loved his singing.

The Memphis Recording Service, a small but lucrative sideline to the Sun Record Company, was founded and operated by Sam Phillips, who was an independent record producer, leasing and selling tapes to other companies. He handled small-time talent, but was hoping and dreaming of someday latching on a "big talent."

It was a Saturday afternoon when Elvis walked into the office of the Memphis Recording Service. The place was full of people waiting to make personal records. Elvis came in with his guitar and told Marion Keisker, the office manager, that he wanted to make a record. She told him he'd have to wait in line and Elvis said okay and sat down. While he waited, a conversation developed that Marion Keisker was to remember years later and narrate often. Elvis said he was a singer.

"What kind of singer are you?" Marion asked.
"I sing all kinds," Elvis replied.
"Who do you sound like?"
"I don't sound like nobody."
"Hillbilly?" Marion asked.
"Yeah, I sing hillbilly."
"Who do you sound like in hillbilly?" Marion persisted.
"I don't sound like nobody."

His turn at the microphone came and Elvis began to sing "My Happiness," a song by one of his favorite singing groups, The Ink Spots. The second song was "That's When the

Mrs. Gladys Presley and son Elvis

Elvis, Priscilla Presley and daughter Lisa Marie

Heartaches Begin," a weepy ballad. On both songs he accompanied himself on his battered guitar.

When Elvis was halfway through his first song, Marion decided to start taping this young man who sounded like nobody else.

"The reason I taped Elvis was this: over and over I remember Sam saying, 'If I could find a white man who had the Negro sound and the Negro feel, I could make a billion dollars.' This is what I heard in Elvis, this . . . what I guess they now call 'soul'; this Negro sound."

When Sam returned to the studio, Marion played the tape through the studio's recording system. Sam said he was impressed, but the kid needed a lot of work. They had Elvis's address, but didn't get in touch with him.

Several months passed and on January 4, 1954, Elvis visited the Memphis Recording Service a second time. Sam was there and Elvis asked if he liked the tapes Marion made of his singing. Sam said he liked the tapes, and he hoped Elvis was getting along, but he couldn't do anything for him right now. Elvis shuffled his feet, nervously ran his hands through his hair and said he wanted to cut another four-dollar record. Elvis made his second "demo," pairing "Casual Love," a ballad, and "I'll Never Stand in Your Way," another country song. Sam was again impressed but still couldn't do anything for Elvis. The raw talent was there but something was missing.

Elvis wanted a musical career but he wasn't exactly counting on one. Besides driving a truck by day, he began to study at night, learning how to be an electrician. His father continued to pack cans of paint in cardboard boxes for a living. His mother took occasional jobs and battled with occasional illness. Life remained unchanged for Elvis.

At the all-night gospel singing, a tradition in the South, Elvis sometimes got up and sang spirituals as a solo vocalist. Singing the songs he loved best Elvis seemed to have found unusual confidence. He kept his eyes closed most of the time when he sang and moved his hips in a manner not associated with spirituals, but later to gain him the name "Elvis the Pelvis."

Sam Phillips introduced Elvis to Scotty Moore, a young guitarist who more than anyone else was to provide and influence much of the "Elvis Presley sound." With Bill Black, bass player, the trio rehearsed for several months trying to develop a style, to evolve something that was different and unique.

After a recording session at Sun, the trio were sitting around drinking Cokes. Elvis picked up his guitar and started banging on it and singing "That's All Right, Mama." He was jumping around the studio, acting the clown. Bill Black started beating on his bass, and Scotty Moore joined in the fun.

The door to the control room was open, and when they were halfway through the clowning, Sam ran out and said, "What in the devil are you doing?" The boys said, "We don't know." Sam said, "Well, find out real quick and don't lose it. Run

Elvis, Priscilla Presley

through it again and let's put it on tape."

What had been recorded in the tiny studio became pop history. It was to be Elvis's first record, his first public exposure to the youth of America. And with his two backup musicians Elvis combined the sounds of white country music and black blues to form what would be called "rockabilly."

In August 1954, "That's All Right, Mama" was released over the airways on station WHBQ in Memphis. Elvis worried about the reception the record would get, and buried himself in a local movie house. The results of the public exposure were very good. Kids called the radio station asking for the record to be played again and again and again.

Within a few days, there were orders for five thousand records, and Sun Record hadn't even cut the master. They gave the radio station a dub, the only existing copy.

Elvis continued working as a truckdriver and on weekends appeared at local night clubs. The record was a regional hit, selling something under twenty thousand copies. *Billboard* called Elvis a "potent new chanter who can sock over a tune for either country or the r&b markets." It was an encouraging beginning but not extraordinary enough to guarantee success.

Many radio stations in the surrounding states refused to play the record, saying it sounded "too black" for them. Nevertheless the record did accomplish more than most first records. It sold well in Memphis, and provided Elvis with some needed money. The record also helped Elvis get on two of the nation's most revered country radio programs, Nashville's *Grand Ole Opry* and Shreveport's *Louisiana Hayride.*

Elvis's appearance on *Grand Ole Opry* wasn't successful. The home of country music wasn't pleased with what they called Elvis's bastardization of their music. The head of the talent office there told Elvis after his performance that he should go back to driving a truck. This piece of criticism broke Elvis's hopeful heart. He left Nashville with tears in his eyes.

The *Louisiana Hayride* radio show had already figured significantly in the careers of several country personalities (Hank Williams among them) and Elvis scored a tremendous hit on the air. The audience accepted his new sound and clamored for more. Elvis was invited back and given a year's contract to appear on the show each week.

By now Elvis had quit his job as truckdriver and was appearing at the Overton Park Shell in Memphis at an all-country-music show. This was the first time Elvis had ever come on stage before a large audience on a commercial show. He had stage presence, a certain ease before the audience, and when he started to shake his hips, he brought the audience to near hysterics—their faces were flushed, mouths opened in shrieking

Tom Jones, Priscilla Presley, Elvis

and screaming bodies tensed, moving, writhing with the sensations of the new beat.

Screaming crowds, favorable votes from disc jockeys, and a contract with *Louisiana Hayride* notwithstanding, things were rough financially. The bookings had been few and literally far apart, with Scotty, Elvis and Bill pushing their car all over the South, working for little more than meal money and gas enough to reach the next village.

In January 1955, Elvis's second record was released, "Good Rockin' Tonight." The record didn't sell as well as the first, rising no higher than number three in Memphis, and hardly appearing in the country music charts in other cities. Elvis's third record, "Milkcow Blues Boogie," also sold poorly. It was beginning to look like his brief success was over.

But Colonel Tom Parker, a flamboyant personal manager, who resembled W. C. Fields and P. T. Barnum, had Elvis under his shrewd gaze. The Colonel was noted as a man with the remarkable ability to recognize talent and promote it successfully. He first saw Elvis in Memphis and knew he had potential. First the Colonel wanted to see how well Elvis would do in the record charts, then he waited for reports from the field—which all called Elvis a "potential smash."

Colonel Parker already had managed two of country music's top singers, Eddy Arnold and Hank Snow. He could wait for Elvis to gain more experience. He made no move or commitment. But he did begin to help Elvis with bookings in the South and Southwest. Elvis was well received everywhere he went.

Elvis and parents

The only rejection Elvis received during this time came when he flew to audition for "Arthur Godfrey's Talent Scouts," then the most popular new talent showcase on television. It was Elvis's first airplane flight and his first time in New York. Elvis didn't like New York and Godfrey didn't like Elvis; the "Talent Scouts" said no. Elvis went back to the live audiences that appreciated his brand of music.

Elvis was energetic, almost to a nervous fault, keeping his closest friends —in those days, Scotty and Bill— awake all night talking and clowning. Elvis chewed his fingernails, drummed his hands against his thighs, tapped his feet, and every chance he got, he'd run a comb through blonde hair that had so much hair cream in it, it looked dark.

It seemed somehow that all this energy was but a prelude to what was coming. Draped in black slacks with a pink stripe down the sides, a pink shirt with the collar turned up catching the ends of his longish hair, a pink sport jacket with big teardrops on the front and back, Elvis would appear on stage. The glaring lights half blinding him, he would lean forward, legs braced, guitar around his neck, hands clutching the stand microphone, and begin to sing. Soon his legs were jerking and twisting and snapping back into the original braced position. His arms flailed the

Vernon Presley, Elvis

guitar, pounding the wood on the afterbeat and snapping strings. He bumped his hips. There were screams and yells from the audience. He'd sneer, drop his eyelids and smile out of the corner of the left side of his mouth. He moved as his music moved him and jumped and turned with near-religious intensity of feeling. Abandoning their seats, the fans jammed around the stage, trying desperately to touch him.

From one song to another, most of them already recorded for Sun or soon to be released, Elvis whipped the fans into hysterics. It was country music with a beat; music that made their behinds itch.

The male population of the audience were mostly jealous and some were filled with hatred for the strutting, swivel-hipped singer. Some would get a gang and try to waylay him after a show. On a few occasions Elvis had to defend himself against physical harm.

In the middle of July 1955, "Baby, Let's Play House" became Elvis's first record to appear on one of the national best-seller charts. The last record for Sun was "Mystery Train." As the record was being shipped to record stores, Colonel Parker decided it was time to move in. The Colonel shrewdly estimated the appeal of Elvis's looks, voice and personality on the growing teenage audience and knew he had a gold mine in the young, greasy-haired, gyrating singer.

The Colonel surveyed the bidders for Elvis's contract and chose RCA Victor. The contract from RCA gave Sun Records $35,000, with another $5,000 going to Elvis. In 1955, $40,000 was an unheard-of sum to pay for a promising artist.

The Colonel and Elvis shook hands and began the most famous manager-artist team in the history of show business. "You stay talented and sexy and I'll make amazing deals that'll make us both rich as rajahs," the Colonel said. And being a man of his word, he made both of them richer than any rajah.

In January 1956, Elvis started to record for RCA the first of the dozens of albums that made him the singing idol of the fifties and early sixties. Elvis's style had evolved in the months since he'd recorded in Memphis. Much of the biting edge of Scotty's guitar and nearly all the pelvic boogie beat had been removed. All the songs were ballads in the first RCA album. Elvis's rhythmic, fluid tenor voice (with a touch of baritone), and the amazing vocal gimmickry remained distinctly his own, but the overall impression was that he had abandoned rockabilly for pop music. The Colonel had begun the gradual transformation of Elvis into a mass-consumption product and superstar.

Elvis was back on the road, plugging away in the South, when it was announced that he had been booked for a series of six Saturday night appearances on the Tommy and Jimmy Dorsey "Stage Show." Mail for the Dorsey show, after Elvis's appearance, far surpassed anything in the program's experience.

When any personality begins to make waves·in the great sea of public recognition, Hollywood sooner or later comes calling. In April 1956, Elvis went to Hollywood for a screen test at Paramount Studios. Hal Wallis, a producer of many successful

The Presley family

and varied films, thought Elvis had what it takes to be a movie star. If the public paid to *hear* Elvis on records, they would surely pay to *see* and hear him on film.

In the screen test Elvis played a scene with veteran character actor Frank Faylen. Elvis wore jeans and a work shirt and was told to run through a few motions like gesturing wildly and feverishly, poking a cigar in the corner of his mouth the next moment as he tapped the old actor on the chest to emphasize a point he'd just made. Of course this had nothing to do with Elvis's appeal to the public. He wasn't singing or performing his specialty of stoking the emotions of his audience, to see how it would reproduce on film. No, the producer wanted to see if Elvis could "act"—as if it really made any difference.

Priscilla Presley, Elvis (at time of divorce, 1973)

Hal Wallis reviewed the test and offered the Colonel a three-picture contract, the first to be made in the fall, possibly in the early winter, depending upon how rapidly a script, director and supporting cast could be arranged. For his services, Elvis was to be paid $100,000, to be increased to $150,000 for the third film.

While in California for the screen test, Elvis made another network appearance, on the Milton Berle show. The show was aired April 3 with an estimated audience of forty million, a figure that represented one out of every four people in the U.S.A.

His records continued to dominate the charts, making it seem as if he were the only singer in the trade. No matter where you looked, it was *Elvis Presley*.

For a long time Elvis's overwhelming popularity with the young obscured the fact that he really had a great singing voice and a fine musical ear. He also had a feel for popular music much greater than other people at that time. He was able to channel it in a direction that kids liked, because that was the way *he* liked it. Elvis has been one of the most influential musicians of the century. He was influenced by all the musical mainstreams of America's subcultures: black and white gospels, country and western, rhythm and blues. In turn, Elvis influenced practically every singer or group that came after him. The British pop singers—the Beatles, the Rolling Stones—who in the early sixties came to America in triumph, were all influenced by Elvis.

"Whirling Dervish of Sex"

"A howling hillbilly success," was the way the headlines read in *Life,* Elvis's first national magazine spread. In Amarillo, Texas, where Elvis had been interviewed for *Life,* girls kicked through a plate-glass door to offer Elvis bits of their underwear to autograph.

Time and *Newsweek* greeted Elvis with columns of hesitant praise. *Time* called him the "teenager's hero," saying his voice was rich and round, his diction poor, and his movements sexy. Teenage girls went wild when they saw him, the magazine said, and as a result Elvis was pocketing $7,500 in profits each week.

As a dutiful and loving son, he bought his parents a $40,000 one-story ranch house in Memphis. The house became a target for Memphis teenagers, so much so that Elvis had a brick wall built to separate the house from the street and then added tall metal spikes—none of which did any good. The fans only trespassed more boldly, pulling up blades of grass from the lawn, pressing their noses against the house windows, and even scraping dust from Elvis's Cadillacs into small envelopes.

The first week in June, Elvis was back in California, making his second appearance on the Milton Berle show. Then he was signed to appear on Steve Allen's new Sunday show being broadcast live from New York.

Yvonne Lime, Elvis in front of Graceland

Elvis, Tempest Storm   Barbara Lang, Elvis

It was after he appeared on the Berle show again on June 6 that Elvis collected some more of the criticism that now seemed as much a part of the act as the wiggle and the voice. Jack Gould, television critic for *The New York Times*, delivered a typical virulent blast:

"Mr. Presley has no discernible singing ability. His specialty is rhythm songs which he renders in an undistinguished whine; his phrasing, if it can be called that, consists of the stereotyped variations that go with a beginner's aria in a bathtub. For the ear he is an unutterable bore.

"From watching Mr. Presley it is wholly evident that his skill lies in another direction. He is a rock-and-roll variation of one of the most standard acts in show business: the virtuoso of the hootchy-kootchy. His one specialty is an accented movement of the body that heretofore has been primarily identified with the repertoire of the blonde bombshells of the burlesque runway."

Jack O'Brien of the New York *Journal-American* was equally unkind: "He can't sing a lick, makes up for vocal shortcomings with the weirdest and plainly planned, suggestive animation short of an aborigine's mating dance."

Nor was this the end of it. During the next few months Elvis appeared on television again and again, and each time the reviews were more anatomical than musical. "Watching him is like watching a stripteaser and a malted milk machine at the same time," commented another critic.

Barbara Hearn, Elvis Presley

Elvis in front of Graceland Manor

Elvis with friends

Elvis with the press at Graceland

Elvis with fans

It was the first of July when Elvis was in New York for the second show of Steve Allen's new series, initiated by NBC in a futile effort to bump off the CBS opposition, Ed Sullivan's "Toast of the Town." Elvis appeared with Imogene Coca and Andy Griffith in a skit, but the real highlight of the show was Elvis singing "Hound Dog."

Steve Allen had Elvis dress in a white-tie-and-tail tuxedo, took away his guitar and told him to stand still while singing. They even positioned a real hound dog on a stool next to Elvis. The dog did nothing but sit and look droopy while Elvis sang to him. Elvis took this attempt at humor in good stride and the adult portion of the audience enjoyed the performance.

The fans did not take it so well. They began picketing the Steve Allen theatre the following morning, carrying signs that said: "We want the real Presley." Meanwhile the TV ratings showed Steve Allen got 55 percent of the viewing audience, while Sullivan was left stumbling around with a miserable 15 percent.

Ed Sullivan quickly began to negotiate for Elvis's appearance on his show. On September 9, Elvis appeared on Sullivan's show, where he cornered 82.6 percent of the audience, which equaled about fifty-four million people, a record that stood until 1964, when Sullivan coaxed the Beatles onto his show.

Elvis's portion of the show—two songs—was broadcast from the CBS Studios in Hollywood as an insert, and Elvis was shown on the home screen from the waist up. The only way anybody at home could tell his

Danny Thomas, Elvis Presley

Judy Powell Spreckles, Elvis

Elvis with fans

Elvis with fan

Elvis with fan

hips were moving was to listen to the screams from the girls in the studio's audience.

Gould wrote in *The New York Times* following Elvis's appearance and complained that Elvis "injected movements of the tongue and indulged in wordless singing that was singularly distasteful." Many people were shocked that such a vulgar spectacle should be allowed into their living rooms via TV.

Always there is something or someone, real or fictional, responsible for the imminent destruction of Society As We Know It. In 1956 it was Elvis the Pelvis, the one-man Sodom and Gomorrah who made love to his guitar, drove the kids up the wall, and frightened their mothers.

All across America the decrees of outrage were posted. In San Antonio, Texas, rock 'n' roll was banished from city swimming pool juke boxes because, according to the city council, the music "attracted undesirable elements given to practicing their spastic gyrations in abbreviated bathing suits." In Asbury Park, New Jersey, newspapers reported that twenty-five "vibrating teenagers" had been hospitalized following a record hop, prompting the mayor to prohibit all future rock concerts in the city's dance halls.

In two Massachusetts towns there were stabbings, and a local district attorney said, "Tin Pan Alley has unleashed a new monster, a sort of nightmare of rhythm. Rock 'n' roll gives young hoodlums an excuse to get together. It inflames teenagers and is obscenely suggestive." The New York *Daily News* said the rioting stretched from "puritanical Boston to julep-loving Georgia," and

Gov. Buford Willington, Elvis

Elvis, Bobby Darin

Elvis relaxing at home

Natalie Wood, Elvis

Elvis, Ann-Margret

accused record makers and disc jockeys of "pandering to the worst juvenile tastes." The paper then recommended a "crackdown on riotous rock 'n' roll"—describing the music as a "barrage of primitive jungle-beat rhythms set to lyrics which few adults would care to hear"—and advocated banning all teenagers from dancing in public without the written consent of their parents, along with a midnight curfew for everyone under twenty-one.

Although men from every professional walk of life joined the massive assault, it was the clergy that seemed the most incensed. The *Catholic Sun* said: "Presley and his voodoo of frustration and defiance have become symbols in our country, and we are sorry to come upon Ed Sullivan in the role of promoter. Your Catholic viewers, Mr. Sullivan, are angry." Evangelist Billy Graham said he'd never met Elvis and didn't know much about him, but, "From what I've heard, I'm not sure I'd want my children to see him." The Reverend Charles Howard Graff of St. John's Episcopal Church called Elvis a "whirling dervish of sex."

Elvis certainly wasn't naive; he was bright enough to know when he'd stumbled onto a good thing, a show-biz gimmick that might win him an enthusiastic following. He also had a lot going for him in 1956—timing, good looks, a rich and versatile singing talent and a crafty manager. Elvis was modest when he told a reporter: "I'm not kiddin' myself. My voice alone is just an ordinary voice. What people come to see is how I use it. If I stand still while I'm singin', I'm dead, man. I might as well go back to drivin' a truck."

Marge Champion, Elvis, Gower Champion

Elvis visiting fan Ellen Marie Mincey in hospital

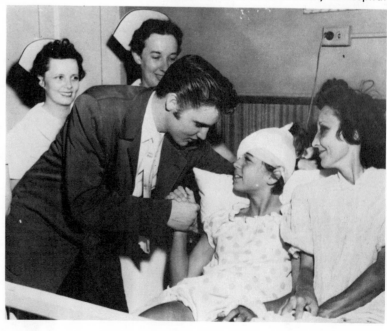

Anita Wood, Elvis

Elvis was many things, but he was not overly aggressive; he was not the egoist many with sudden wealth and fame become. Bold and brutish on stage, off-stage he was a mild and polite person. He owned a fleet of Cadillacs and a small parking lot full of other assorted vehicles. He had a wardrobe that included thirty sport coats and forty sport shirts, and his fingers and wrists glittered with enough diamonds and star sapphires to ransom an Arab oil sheik; but this wasn't ostentation in the usual sense. It was just his way of conforming to the customs of that peculiar cultural group—the successful country and western singers, who flaunted their new wealth with childish glee.

When you put it all together, it made perfect newspaper copy—and Elvis had been cast in the perfect mold. He was six feet tall and quick to punch someone who got out of line. His hair was worn long and slicked back and his sideburns came all the way down to his ears. He rolled the sleeves of his short-sleeved sport shirts three times to show his biceps, wore his collar up in back and slipped a half-inch leather belt into two-inch loops and shoved the buckle over one hip. He liked to drive flashy cars, race motorcycles, shoot pool and make love to girls. Every teenage male wanted to be like him, and legions of them began to imitate him. He was one of the great fantasy figures of the fifties.

The attacks on Elvis continued, and he became a convenient whipping-boy for all the changes that were rippling through the nation. The fan magazines replied to the attacks on their idol with the archetypical de-

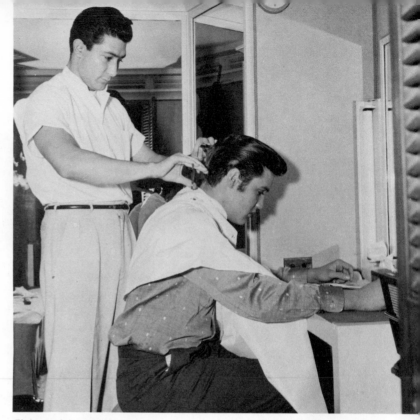

Elvis and hairstylist

Elvis in recording studio

Elvis with fans

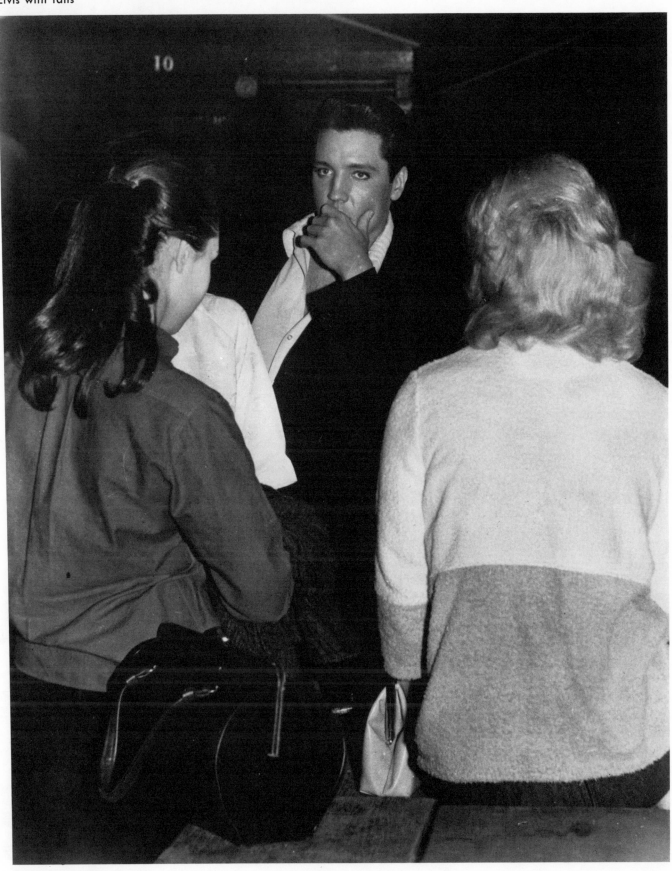

fense of youth throughout the ages: "We are what we are because of the world our parents made." An excellent example comes from one specialty fan magazine that was devoted entirely to Elvis Presley: "There are those who maintain that Elvis Presley is a corrupting influence on society. But art and music reflect our events, they do not cause the chaos of civilization. If our teenagers are wild, primitive, and thrill-seeking, it is the result of an uncertain world caused by the neurotic adults who are trying to place the blame on their children. Presley is the spokesman for the youth. He cries out against injustice of the "generation that goofed," leaving teenagers with war, drafts, national debts and insecurity. His cry is echoed by the crowds. Presley personifies the public."

Elvis never publicly admitted to being a spokesman for anybody, and, contrary to his rebellious image, he was fairly conservative in his views. He looked upon himself only as an entertainer. "For me a stage is a place where I go to work and sing— not where I talk about things of life."

It would be years before the critics reconciled themselves to the Elvis Presley phenomenon and welcomed him to their bosoms. By then, the pop scene was overcrowded with strange-sounding names and even stranger public behavior. By then, Elvis was no longer the "sensuous cyclone," losing gale force as he walked through thirty films that would have vanquished lesser idols into oblivion, recording dozens of albums of almost pure hokum.

Liberace, Elvis

Movie Star

Elvis Presley's film career began in a blaze of controversy. Famous and infamous as a "swivel-hip teenage idol singing sensation," Elvis had the biggest and most avid audience in the world before he ever made a film. The whole teenage world was waiting to see Elvis in Technicolor and CinemaScope and all those cinematic marvels designed with the likes of him in mind.

His voice on records had reached more people than that of any performing artist in the history of the record industry. Singlehandedly he banished country music from the nation's airwaves and replaced it with rock 'n' roll. Guitar sales climbed astronomically, and every youth who wanted to be in fashion *had* to have a guitar, whether he could play or not.

Elvis also changed the style of stardom, making it, among other things, more commercial than it previously had been, while establishing once and for all the enormous weight and power of the "youth market." Under the Colonel's promotion there appeared almost a hundred merchandising items with Elvis's name on it: Elvis Presley bobby socks, shoes, pencils, bubble gum cards, diaries, charm bracelets, pens, shirts, blouses, sweaters, pajamas. If that didn't appeal to you, then there were other choices: belts, ties, stuffed hound dogs and teddy bears, greeting cards, and an Elvis Presley picture that glowed in the dark.

Elvis Presley, Dolores Hart
on the set of "King Creole"

Michael Curtiz, Hal Wallis, Elvis Presley
on the set of "King Creole"

Ann-Margret, Elvis Presley on the set of "Viva Las Vegas"

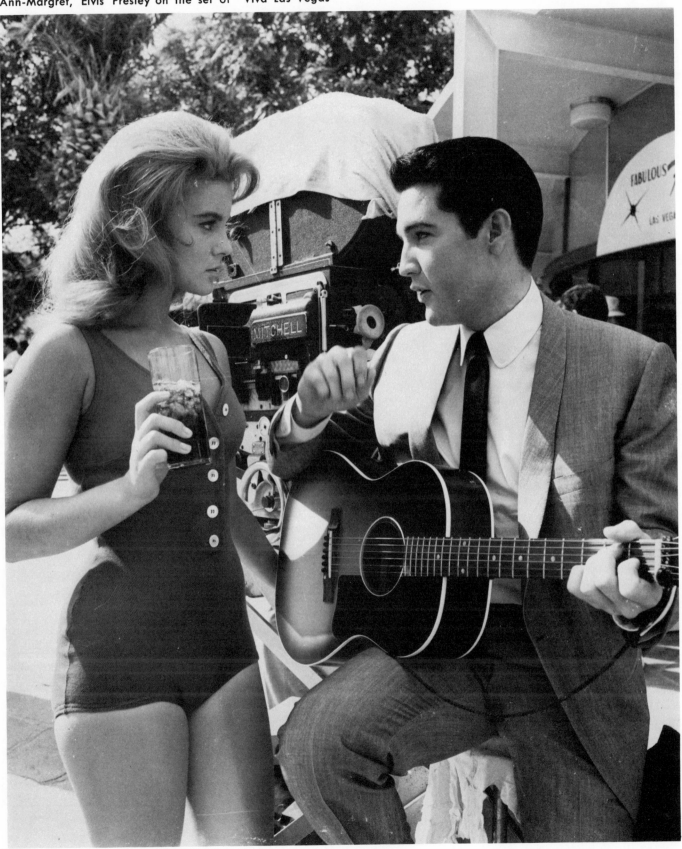

Through Elvis an obvious, healthy, and good-natured sexuality was added to the popular music scene. There had been a total ban on sex in pop music before Elvis came along and put action to the words he sang. So far as the teenage female was concerned, Elvis Presley was Rudy Vallee, Rudolph Valentino, Clark Gable, and Frank Sinatra all wrapped into one.

Elvis began work on his first film— a western, *Love Me Tender*—in August 1957. Originally the film was titled *The Reno Brothers* and there were no songs, but when it became apparent that Elvis represented enormous box-office potential, four tunes were hurriedly added to the shaky script and the title of the film was changed to *Love Me Tender*—so the film would get a free plug whenever the record was played.

In the film, Elvis had three brothers, the oldest played by Richard Egan, and according to the plot, everybody but Elvis goes off to fight for the South during the Civil War, leaving Elvis back home on the farm to look after Mom. Word comes that Egan is dead, and Elvis and Debra Paget marry. Debra had been Egan's fiancée before he was "killed," although Elvis doesn't know that. Then Egan returns and it gets complicated until Elvis solves the problem by dying dramatically. It was a terrific debut, but there was no rock 'n' roll in the film. Fans were disappointed but nevertheless flocked to see their idol.

Usually two or three hundred prints of a film are released at one time, but when *Love Me Tender* was

Elvis Presley
wardrobe test on "Love Me Tender"

Paul Stewart, Dick Winslow, Elvis Presley,
Jan Shepard ("King Creole")

Ursula Andress, Elvis Presley
on the set of "Fun in Acapulco"

ready for the nation's theaters, no less than 550 prints were ordered. Within three weeks the million dollars of the film's cost had been recovered. Never before had any Hollywood film gotten its money back so rapidly.

The producer of *Love Me Tender* was David Weisbart, who had been producer of James Dean's most popular film, *Rebel Without a Cause,* in 1955. Because Dean was the only other true teen idol to emerge in the 1950s, numerous comparisons were made. On Elvis's first day on the set, part of the talk between Elvis and his producer was devoted to whether he might not be right for the leading role when Hollywood got around to producing *The James Dean Story,* a film concept much discussed in 1956, the year following Dean's tragic death. Elvis said he thought he could handle the assignment.

"So far as teenagers are concerned, Elvis is what I call a safety valve," Weisbart said. "By that I mean they scream, holler, articulate, and let go of their emotions when they see him perform. But when they watched Jimmy Dean perform they bottled their emotions and were sort of sullen and brooding. Elvis is completely outgoing, where Jimmy was the direct opposite.

"Both boys were immature, but it was not as easy to spot it in Jimmy, who was an introvert. Part of Elvis's great charm lies in his immaturity. I never got an uneasy feeling about Elvis, because on the surface he seemed to be open and impulsive, but Jimmy was never open, never did anything impulsively.

Juliet Prowse, Hal Wallis, Elvis Presley on the set of "G.I. Blues"

Elvis Presley, Ursula Andress, director Richard Thorpe on the set of "Fun in Acapulco"

Shirley MacLaine, Elvis Presley
on the set of "G.I. Blues"

"Elvis was by far the more healthy. Jimmy was apparently the typical confused teenager, but Elvis is something every kid would like to be—a phenomenal success without having to work for it. He's up there enjoying himself and getting millions of dollars. According to a child's logic, what could be better?"

The critics welcomed Elvis's film debut with words like "turgid" and "juicy" to describe his characterization, noting: ". . . dramatic contribution is not a great deal more impressive than that of the slavering nags." But it was up to *Time* to go overboard in being cruelly cute with the following review:

"Is it a sausage? It is certainly smooth and damp-looking, but who ever heard of a 172-pound sausage six feet tall? Is it a Walt Disney goldfish? It has the same sort of big, soft, beautiful eyes and long, curly lashes, but who ever heard of a goldfish with sideburns? Is it a corpse? The face just hangs there, limp and white with its little drop-seat mouth.

"But suddenly the figure comes to life. The lips part, the eyes half close, the clutched guitar begins to undulate back and forth in an uncomfortably suggestive manner. And wham! The midsection of the body jolts forward to bump and grind and beat out a low-down rhythm that takes its pace from boogie and hillbilly rock 'n' roll and something known only to Elvis and his Pelvis. A peculiar sound emerges. A rusty foghorn? A voice? Words occasionally can be made out . . . 'Goan . . . git . . . luhhv . . .' And then all at once everything stops, and a big

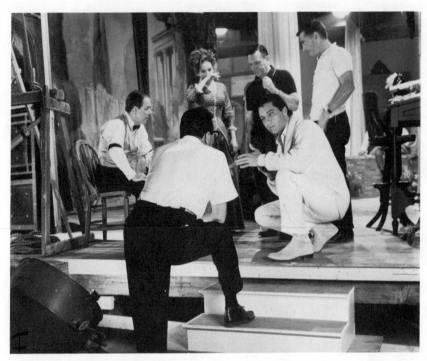

Elvis with crew and cast of "Frankie and Johnny"

trembly tender half smile, half sneer smears slowly across the CinemaScope screen. The message that millions of U.S. teenage girls love to receive has just been delivered."

Most other critics felt the same about Elvis's debut. For someone who wanted to be an actor, it was not a promising debut. But the critics' sarcasm was wasted on the paying audience and the studio heads. Elvis was big box office, an instantly bankable star.

Elvis started to work on his second film, *Loving You,* at Paramount, co-starring with Lizabeth Scott and Wendell Corey. This was the first of nine films Hal Wallis made with Elvis and the first of several espe-

Lizabeth Scott, Elvis Presley
on the set of ''Loving You''

cially written for Elvis and based loosely on his own rags-to-riches story. It was also the first film where Elvis could be seen in glorious Technicolor by his fans.

Elvis arrived in New York for his third and final appearance on the Ed Sullivan show and the streets were blocked off for seven blocks around the theatre. About five thousand kids stood around screaming. They had policemen on horses directing the human traffic, trying to keep the crowds under control.

Elvis appeared in a gold lamé suit with a black satin lining and a velvet shirt, singing a religious song that was to be on his next record album, *Peace in the Valley*. It was his last TV appearance for more than three years.

In May 1957, Elvis was to begin filming his third film, *Jailhouse Rock*, for MGM. The price tag was $250,000 plus 50% of all profits.

A few months previous, Elvis bought a $100,000 estate, Graceland, near Memphis. The house, two stories tall, built of tan Tennessee limestone with tall, white Colonial pillars outside, was to be the home of the rising King of Films. The mansion had twenty-three rooms and was situated on a hilltop in the middle of a thirteen-acre plot surrounded by rolling grazing land. Down from the house, at the ten-foot wrought-iron Graceland gates, with their larger-than-life-size metal figures of Elvis playing the guitar, the fans were in constant attendance. Graceland became Memphis's number-one tourist attraction.

Richard Thorpe, Elvis Presley
on the set of "Fun in Acapulco."
Elvis eyes the shooting schedule as
director Richard Thorpe points

Juliet Prowse, Elvis Presley,
director Norman Taurog
on the set of "G.I. Blues"

Barbara Stanwyck, Elvis Presley
on the set of "Roustabout"

"You're in the Army Now"

Elvis was twenty-three years old, in excellent health, making more money than the governor of his own home state, and was a budding movie star. He also was the number-one rock 'n' roll singer, over whom thousands of girls screamed, fainted and mauled themselves, every time he performed in public.

Then a letter arrived from Uncle Sam. Elvis was ordered to report to the Memphis draft board office on January 20, 1958. For months previously there were rumors and speculations on Elvis's drafting. Army and Navy recruiters visited Elvis' to offer him special enlistment opportunities. The Navy even went so far as to say that it would form an "Elvis Presley Company" with boys from Memphis if Elvis would sign the Navy enlistment papers. Elvis thanked everybody and said he'd take his chances with the draft.

If Elvis was treating everything matter-of-factly, Paramount Pictures and Hal Wallis in Hollywood were ready to climb the walls in panic. Elvis had been scheduled to report for his next film the same week the Army wanted him, and $350,000 already had been committed to the project, all of which would be lost, they said, if Elvis went into the Army before March.

The studio and Elvis requested a delay until March 20, and were unanimously granted a sixty-day deferment. Elvis said he was grateful—"for the studio's sake."

The Presleys visit Elvis in the service

But the fans felt very differently. In the last days of 1957, the three-man draft board in Memphis became one of the most unpopular in the entire country. First there were the fans, who began writing letters and calling to complain about Elvis's being drafted to begin with. Other fans circulated petitions calling for Elvis to be named a "national treasure" and protected from the draft. "Would you draft Beethoven?" one fan asked. And then there were those who didn't like Elvis to start with, calling to complain about giving the no-good, greasy-haired, hip-wriggling singer a deferment.

Elvis returned to Hollywood in January 1958, to begin work on *King Creole,* which was loosely based on the Harold Robbins novel, *A Stone for Danny Fisher.* Thanks in large part to the director, Michael Curtiz (who in his heyday at Warner Bros. directed every Warner star of the '30s and '40s), and with flashes of brilliance by Carolyn Jones and Walter Matthau, the film is among Elvis's best.

On a cold, rainy Monday morning, March 24, 1958, Elvis arrived at

Elvis, arriving at Fort Hood, Texas

Local Draft Board 86. Already dozens of newsmen and photographers were there. Elvis's parents were there and so was the Colonel, who was handing out balloons that advertised Elvis's upcoming film, *King Creole.*

Photographers trailed along, popping bulbs every time he stepped before another examining officer. Then Elvis was sworn in, designated US 53310761, and then boarded a chartered bus for Fort Chaffee, Arkansas. For the next two years, he was the most famous soldier in the world.

Much thought and newspaper space had been given to Elvis's entrance into the Armed Forces and what it meant to his career. On one side there were the paper prophets who said it was the end of his reign as pop music king. They said that not only would he suffer a rather noticeable cut in salary—from $100,000 to $78 a month—he also would be unable to defend his position against other singers who were not so rigidly restricted. He would be unable to make any movies and it was unlikely he could do any concerts. And when dealing with the fickleness of pop culture, two years is a long time. The critics said Elvis was dead, and all that was missing was the funeral.

"Not so," said the Colonel. Certainly Elvis wasn't going to miss any payments on anything he was buying. There was that thousand dollars a week coming in from RCA, a contractual clause the Colonel had put in—Elvis was to be paid a thousand a week, whether or not he worked. Paramount owed him 50% of all profits from *King Creole,* as yet unreleased, and it was regarded as a sure thing that the film would make millions, it being the only way Elvis was going to be seen until 1960. Not

After being issued seventy-five pounds of G.I. gear, Elvis was shipped to Fort Hood, Texas for basic training where he was an exemplary recruit, enjoying the competitiveness and tolerating the regimentation as best he could. He had to live with his fellow soldiers, who kidded him endlessly—"Maybe you'd like rock 'n' roll instead of reveille." The press was removed from Elvis's life but the fans still persisted. Some swarmed over the post on weekends, hoping for a glimpse of their idol.

Everybody expected Elvis to take the easy route—going into the Army's Special Service branch, where he could sing his way through his tour of duty. Even the Army half expected Elvis to request the Special Service branch, where he might appear in television commercials to boost enlistment, as well as entertaining at military installations and selling a few bonds, as so many other drafted singers did.

But Elvis publicly said he didn't want any special treatment. The Colonel also knew that this path served his own purpose, that if Elvis carried a rifle and drove a truck for two years, rather than sing, the adult acceptance for Elvis would multiply vastly. The Colonel wanted a much larger audience for Elvis than teenagers. He wanted the whole wide world.

In late May, *King Creole* was released and the critics, for the first time, liked Elvis in a picture. *Billboard* said it was Elvis's "best acting performance to date." *The New York Times* film critic Howard Thompson said, "Elvis Presley can act."

only were there several songs already recorded and ready for release as singles, but it was believed several more would be cut if necessary. Army regulations regarding off-duty activities by military personnel were broad enough to make it fairly easy for Elvis to turn out more records.

Besides the lipsticks and T-shirts and other novelties that continued to sell, now that Elvis was in the Army it only increased the already broad range of product possibilities. Novelty songs about Elvis made an appearance—"Dear 53310761," "Bye Bye Elvis," "Mar-chin' Elvis," and "All-American Boy."

The famous head of hair and long sideburns were cut into the close-cropped G.I. style. The Colonel had the fallen hair collected and sent out to fan clubs all over the country.

After basic and advanced training at Fort Hood, Texas, Elvis and 1,400 soldiers were ready to be replacements to the Third Armored Division in Germany.

On August 14, 1958, Elvis's mother died at the age of forty-six, of a heart attack. Elvis was granted emergency leave and rushed home. There were sixty-five city policemen hired to handle the traffic and pedestrian problems at the funeral service, as reporters, photographers and fans crushed forward, pushing rudely, taking in every sob and mumbled syllable, as their idol mourned his idolized mother.

"We were always an affectionate family," Elvis stated. "My mother was the most wonderful person in the world. I always felt a little bit lonely, maybe a better word would be incomplete, when I was little. But I could tell my mother about it, how I felt and she'd talk to me, and then the feeling would go away. I suppose it might have been different if my brother had lived. A lot of things might have been different. But he didn't live, and I grew up alone. I guess my mother—and my father, too, of course—were trying to make up for that by giving me enough love for both."

In New York reporters waited for the train from Texas which was bringing Elvis and the other troops scheduled for overseas duty. Finally Elvis appeared, dressed in khakis and wearing a garrison cap pulled down over but not hiding hair that had been bleached by the hot Texas sun. A noisy press conference was held and at the conclusion, with the Army band doing its best to make

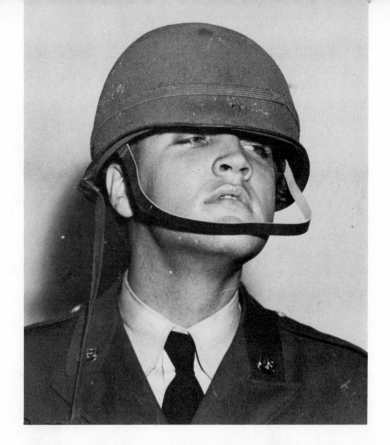

Elvis's Army Induction Physical

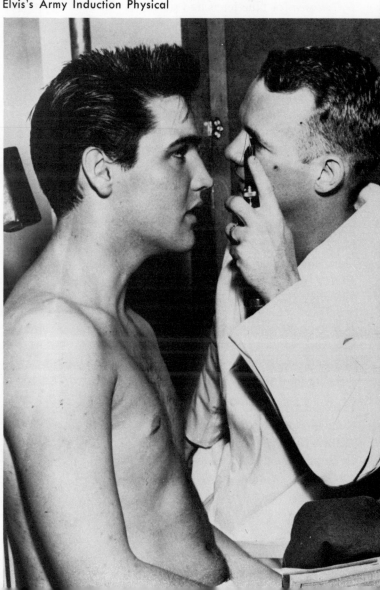

"Hound Dog" sound like a Sousa march, the press departed and Elvis and the rest of the 1,400 soldiers boarded the troopship *General Randell* and sailed for Bremerhaven, Germany.

Elvis was no stranger in Germany. His records sold briskly to German youth. Even a German-style Elvis—Peter Kraus—was doing well in Deutschland. Now the real thing was headed their way. There even arose a magazine, *Bravo,* today one of the world's largest youth publications, due to Elvis's popularity in Germany.

Germany's youth, mere infants when World II ended, became Americanized quickly. They abandoned their *lederhosen* for blue jeans and started standing and walking like cowboys. Bored with traditional German music, they turned to American rock 'n' roll. Elvis Presley was just what they were looking for—an American Pied Piper to lead them to excitement. German girls could scream and shriek and faint just as well as any American girl.

Of course, not all of Germany was thrilled about Elvis's visit. A German archaeologist said Elvis was a throwback to the Stone Age. And one German disc jockey destroyed all Elvis's records and called him a "howling dog."

However, the handwriting was on the wall; in fact, over many walls, German fans proclaimed: *Elvis über alles!* in bold painted strokes.

Five hundred adoring, screaming teenagers, most of them shouting, "Ellllvvviiisss!," waited at the dock in Bremerhaven on October 1, and spotted Elvis coming down the gangplank, even though he, like the other troops, was dressed in Army fatigues

and carried a heavy duffel bag. The Army positioned a troop train near the ship's unloading area and Elvis and the others were on their way to Friedberg, their Army post, before the fans grew hoarse with screaming.

The press reception at the post was a rerun of earlier confrontations, the only difference being an international press corps, asking the same old questions in a half-dozen accents.

Elvis was permitted to live off the post under the military sponsoring act—governing a soldier's living with dependents and relatives.

Initially it was rumored that Elvis and his father were looking for a castle to live in. Later they settled for a four-bedroom, two-story, middle-class German house that needed repairs and boasted an exorbitant rent—some five times what a German would pay.

No sooner had Elvis settled down to become a well-greased gear in the Army machine, when an ill wind blew in from the Iron Curtain.

If the middle-aged citizenry of the U.S.A. viewed Elvis with misgivings, the East German Communists looked upon Elvis as a calculated plot to undermine the morals of Communist youth and as an act of provocation by NATO forces. The official Communist Party newspaper, *Neues Deutschland,* published a picture of Elvis with a sixteen-year-old German girl, whom he dated a couple of times, and called him a "Cold War Weapon," saying: "Puffed up like a peacock, Presley, hooting like a ship-warning buoy, is an advertisement for NATO in the East Zone." Another East German paper criticized Elvis's voice—bluntly stating he had none—and continued: "Those persons plotting an atomic war are making a fuss about Presley because they know youth dumb enough to become Presley fans are dumb enough to fight in the war."

The Communist press viewed tight pants and bootleg jazz—a reference to the Elvis Presley songs still being recorded on discarded X-ray plates— as the first steps toward degradation and crime. If anyone demanded proof, the Communists had it. A leader of a juvenile gang arrested in Halle, East Germany, was described as having gone wrong after buying several Presley records and hanging a signed picture of Elvis in his living room. Police in Leipzig were arresting members of another gang who, they claimed, had fallen under the influence of "NATO ideology" and had committed anti-state acts; the name of the gang was the "Elvis Presley Hound Dogs."

Back in West Germany, it was business as usual. According to Elvis's sergeant, he "scrubbed, washed, greased, painted, marched, ran, carried his laundry and worried through inspections just as everyone else did." At times he sang informally for his Army buddies, practiced Karate, and met his future wife—Priscilla Beaulieu, then a young teenager. Elvis was promoted from Private First Class to Specialist Fourth Class and by January 1960 was a buck sergeant. In another month, he would be discharged.

A series of newspaper articles reviewing the past and previewing the future began appearing from coast to coast. Fan magazines were announcing contests offering Elvis's uniforms as prizes. Two hundred prints of *Jailhouse Rock,* which had grossed close to four million dollars the first

Elvis inducted into the Army

Elvis, Tina Louise

Elvis with fans

58

time around, were pushed to movie theatres for an early March opening. Radio stations in cities across the nation planned special programs that took the shape of Elvis marathons. Again, a rush of novelty songs appeared—"I'm Gonna Hang Up My Rifle," "The King Is Coming Back."

Elvis's first public appearance was scheduled for one of Frank Sinatra's TV shows; Elvis would be paid $125,000.

The excitement was honestly motivated. Elvis was still the reigning monarch of the pop music charts, and it was a triumphant return to the U.S. During his absence, much had happened. Jerry Lee Lewis had been banished by the prudish public after marrying his thirteen-year-old cousin. Buddy Holly, Richie Valens and the Big Bopper were dead. Rock 'n' roll was reeling from a payola probe. The top album sellers in the winter of 1959–60 were Ricky Nelson, Frankie Avalon, Fabian and Bobby Darin, all Elvis Presley imitators. No one had come along during Elvis's tour of duty to upset his throne as King of Rock 'n' Roll.

The Mississippi legislature passed a resolution saying he had become "a legend and inspiration to tens of millions of Americans and hence reaffirms an historic American ideal that success in our nation can still be attained through individual initiative, hard work and abiding faith in one's self and in the Creator."

From a greasy-haired, vulgar, hip-wriggling singer, Elvis became the all-American prototype, the Horatio Alger hero of the South: the son of a dirt-poor sharecropper who sang in his mama's church and went on to massive wealth and fame.

Elvis with fan

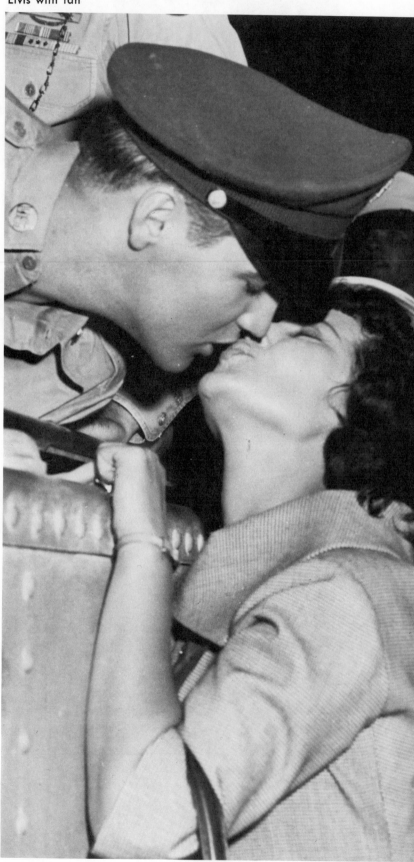

Homecoming

On March 5, 1960, Elvis was once more a civilian. After a press conference in Germany, there was another one at McGuire Air Force Base in New Jersey. While the press conference went on inside, outside in a blizzard, scratching on the windows and shouting pledges of undying love, were a couple of hundred teenagers.

The train trip to Memphis was indicative of the nature of the following months. In every little town along the way the tracks were lined, twenty-four hours a day, with photographers, cameramen and kids. In some towns, the Colonel and Elvis stood on the train's rear platform, as if Elvis were running for President, waving and singing autographs.

Arriving in Memphis, Elvis was met by crowds so large that police had to escort him to Graceland, causing a monstrous traffic jam.

The first days were spent calling friends, reassembling the old gang, lying around, looking at the house he hadn't seen in more than eighteen months, making plans for remodeling. Then, on March 28, Elvis drove to Nashville for the first recording session. Among the songs recorded in that all-night session were "Stuck on You," and "Fame and Fortune," ballads for which there were more than a million orders before Elvis opened his mouth.

The next day Elvis caught the train for Miami Beach, where Frank Sinatra would be videotaping his

Frank Sinatra, Elvis Presley

show. It was ironic that Elvis should make his return debut on Sinatra's show, for in 1957, Sinatra denounced rock 'n' roll as "phony and false, and sung, written and played for the most part by cretinous goons." There was, however, a motive in booking Elvis—a *guaranteed* high score in the all-important TV ratings.

Elvis was in rehearsals and showed considerable nervousness. It was agreed that he'd wear a tuxedo and stand still while singing, as a concession to the Sinatra image of sophistication.

Despite the Colonel's efforts to include a teenage crowd, more than half the audience was composed of affluent middle-aged Sinatra fans. Here were idols from two different generations, on stage at the same time, and singing. Elvis sang both sides of his new single, then sang one of Sinatra's songs, "Witchcraft," after which Sinatra sang one of Elvis's, "Love Me Tender," with Elvis joining him in harmony. Eighteen years had passed since Sinatra's bobby-soxers swooned in the aisles of the Paramount Theatre in New York; two years had gone by since Elvis was causing riots in every city he appeared. Now they were together, and the audience came unglued, loving every moment.

Critically, it was received less ecstatically. "The expected dynamite was, to put it politely, a bit overrated," said *Billboard. The New York Times* was rougher: "The recent liberation from the Army of Elvis Presley may have been one of the most irritating events since the invention of itching powder."

Elvis, Bill Black (in background)

Following the Sinatra special, Elvis returned to Nashville for a recording session lasting twelve hours, during which he recorded twelve songs, all released a week later on an album titled *Elvis Is Back*. Fans greeted the album jubilantly.

Elvis traveled to Hollywood in style, renting a private railroad car for the trip. Elvis was ready to resume his movie career, and the studios were more than ready to produce Elvis Presley films, in other words, money-making films.

Paramount went into production with *G.I. Blues,* which had an Army story line. The background scenes and second-unit work were filmed in Germany during Elvis's tour of duty. Visitors to the Paramount set during the shooting of *G.I. Blues* included the wife and daughter of the Brazilian president, the king and queen of Thailand, and princesses from Denmark, Norway and Sweden. Each claimed to be an avid Elvis fan.

In July, RCA released Elvis's second post-Army single, "It's Now or Never," a song that was based on the popular "O Sole Mio." The song occupied the number-one slot for five weeks. Since it was a non-rocker, it played on many more stations normally unaccustomed to playing Elvis's records. This fact was noticed by RCA and the Colonel, and the next single released was even further away from the rock 'n' roll beat.

The people who expected Elvis to return to the image of greasy-haired, hip-shaking arrogance and the blaring rock 'n' roll beat were disappointed. The once-famous sideburns did not reappear once he returned from the Army. Neither did the rock 'n' roll.

If there was any doubt, one only had to see *G.I. Blues,* released simultaneously in more than five hundred theatres in October. In the film Elvis not only worked with puppets but with small children. Although there were a few rockers in the soundtrack, most of the songs sounded as if their roots were in Tin Pan Alley rather than in country blues.

"When they took the boy out of the country, they apparently took the country out of the boy," said the *Hollywood Reporter.* "It is a subdued and changed Elvis Presley who has returned from military service in Germany to star in Hal Wallis's *G.I. Blues."* Bosley Crowther of *The New York Times* was amazed at how wholesome Elvis had become, saying Elvis had honey in his veins instead of red, hot blood.

Regardless of the critics, the movie was a box-office success, and by the time *G.I. Blues* was released, Elvis was making a film at 20th Century-Fox, *Flaming Star.* In this, his second western, Elvis played the half-breed son of a Kiowa Indian and a white rancher.

Don Siegel, director of the film, agreed to have Elvis sing the title song over the credits, and one song at a birthday party in the first few minutes of the film. That was the extent of Elvis's singing.

Elvis's fans came to hear him sing, and when he didn't, walked out in disappointment to spread the word to other fans.

"I think the studio made a mistake," said Siegel. "They should have put on a campaign emphasizing that Elvis emerged as an actor in the film. If they weren't going to sell it properly, they shouldn't have released it."

Elvis at recording session during "Jailhouse Rock"

Elvis and his band on the "Ed Sullivan Show"

Elvis at concert (1956)

66

The film was rushed into release faster than any other, opening nationwide, in time for the Christmas school holidays, a pattern that would become as much a part of the Colonel's policy in the release of future films as his reluctance to grant any interviews.

The Colonel was processing thirty thousand Elvis Presley fan letters a month in 1960 (there were five thousand fan clubs worldwide), and he knew that many of the letter writers went to see Elvis's films time after time. Film releases timed with a school vacation would make it easier for these fans to attend the movies on week nights as well as weekends.

From *Flaming Star*, Elvis went into *Wild in the Country*, the last film he made for 20th Century-Fox. The story was about a potential literary talent who had to overcome his rural beginnings, lack of education, and a proclivity for violence. This is one of Elvis's least-remembered films because it is not the typical film he is identified with. The film boasted a good supporting cast: Hope Lange, Tuesday Weld, Millie Perkins, John Ireland and Gary Lockwood. It also was the last film Elvis enjoyed making, and remained one of his personal favorites.

In 1961 Elvis flew to Hawaii to make his last public appearance until 1969. It was a benefit to raise money for the Memorial Fund of the USS *Arizona*. For the next eight years Elvis stayed in his Bel Air mansion or his Memphis hilltop home. For all practical purposes, he went into princely seclusion. His fans could see him only on film and listen to him on records.

Elvis at the Hotel International

Elvis had never been exactly addicted to the Hollywood social scene. There was no open socializing with co-workers, and no personal appearances even at the premieres of his own movies. This was partly due to his shyness and to the fact that Elvis could not appear in public without hysterical crowds gathering.

Elvis's life was divided into making films, cutting records and living a totally insulated social life. In the 1960s he had an entourage of seven to twelve young men of approximately his own age, all of whom were on salary. Most went wherever Elvis went and most were from Memphis. They became the "Memphis Mafia," as the newspapers called them. It was this "Mafia" that gave Elvis, until he married, security, comfort and companionship.

The "Mafia" were on call twenty-four hours a day, three hundred and sixty-five days a year. The relationship was more feudal—a lord and his serfs—than employer and employee. But Elvis was a kind and generous and good-hearted feudal master. "You can live ten lifetimes before you'd find another like him," said an ex-member.

"I have no need for bodyguards," Elvis once said, "but I have very specific uses for two highly trained certified public accountants; an expert transportation man to handle travel arrangements, make reservations, take care of luggage; a wardrobe man; and a confidential aide and a security man who will handle safety arrangements in large cities when crowds of people are involved. This is my corporation which travels with me at all times. More than that,

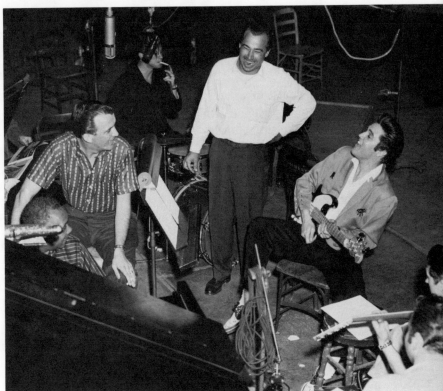

Elvis and musicians during recording session

all these members of my corporation are my friends."

The boys lived with Elvis's moods, which were brought on by the dulling routine of endless films and records, and dieting. Elvis had weird eating habits—burnt bacon, olives, vegetable soup, peanut butter and banana sandwiches. He was constantly worrying about his weight. He'd run his movies and watch himself on the screen, slumping down in his seat, cringing, saying, "No . . . no . . . too fat!"

Good-natured as Elvis was, his temper would flare up occasionally and shake up everyone near him. One time he fired every one of his "Mafia," told them to get the hell out of his sight—permanently. They packed and left. But by the time they got to the airport, Elvis changed his mind. He called the airport and told his entourage to get back in a hurry, they were on the payroll again. On two occasions, when his uncles strayed away from the Graceland gate, Elvis ordered his limousine backed across the highway and driven at high speed *through* the gate.

Most of the time, the "Mafia" led a life that took on the appearance of a young boy's fantasies come true. They would ride motorcycles in packs, calling themselves "El's Angels," clown around, play football, and hold open house parties on weekends. There was an endless supply of girls, mostly in their teens and early twenties, mostly the starlet types. Elvis lived like a rajah, surrounded by an ever-changing harem of admiring females.

"It was weird," said one of the girls. "We'd sit around watching television—that's what we did seventy-five per cent of the time—and nobody'd ever laugh at anything unless Elvis did. If Elvis laughed, everybody'd just roar. Not more than Elvis laughed, but just as much."

For seven years the routine was the same until chronology lost all meaning to Elvis and the people near him. The days and the months and the years all seemed the same.

"It was like when you're stoned and nothing changes," said one of the partying girls. "They could be dropping the atomic bomb and you're inside Elvis's life and it doesn't matter. It just goes on and on."

Singing, Dancing, Romancing Puppet

Elvis, Scotty Moore

From the spring of 1961 to the summer of 1968, Elvis starred in no less than twenty-one films, an average of three a year. Many were so similar that it was difficult to tell them apart. His acting range, as a critic said, was "somewhere between early celluloid and late plastic." At the height of Elvis's popularity, the movie moguls placed him in movies that had some pretense to dramatic presentation. The fans at that time would gladly have been content with Elvis singing and doing nothing else. When he became an established fixture in films, when his dramatic appeal might have been stronger, the movies produced were all non-acting musicals. When he should have been developing as an actor and singer, Elvis was stagnating in some of the most forgettable films made in America. Though he never lost the title of "King," it was an empty crown that was worn during much of the 1960s.

Near the beginning of this period was *Blue Hawaii*. The film had him playing a rich man's son who returns from the service and much against his parents' wishes takes a job with a tourist agency. In *Blue Hawaii*, Elvis was to become the prototype of the "beach movie hero," the type that was to appear in dozens of low-budget beach pictures in the sixties. The film was released for the Thanksgiving-Christmas holidays, and when it completed its run of five hundred theatres in the U.S.A., in early 1962, it had grossed 4.7 million dollars. The soundtrack album became the fastest selling album of 1961.

Elvis's next film was for United Artists, called *Follow That Dream*, where he played the well-meaning but bumbling member of a shiftless family living off the government. It was the first film to take advantage of Elvis's natural flair for comedy.

No sooner was that film finished, than Elvis had turned boxer to star in a remake of the 1933 film, *Kid Galahad*—cleverly retitled *Kid Galahad*. The film was the third in a row in which Elvis often appeared stripped to the waist, something producers apparently believed was an important plus, something the fans could moan and scream about between songs.

Elvis's third movie role in 1962 was that of a charter boat captain in *Girls! Girls! Girls!,* who chased girls while singing thirteen songs. The soundtrack was a big seller.

In 1963, Elvis made four musicals, the first taking him to Seattle for *It Happened at the World's Fair*. He plays a bush pilot whose co-pilot keeps getting into gambling trouble. Elvis chases Yvonne Craig and winds up with Joan O'Brien in the picture, while singing ten songs.

Fun in Acapulco was a more substantial film, giving Elvis a solid story line about a trapeze artist afraid of heights after an accident in the States. The scenery was picture-postcard beautiful, something many of Elvis's films offered. In the end, after singing about a dozen songs and romancing Ursula Andress, Elvis dives from a monstrous cliff and loses his fear of heights. The soundtrack was another best-selling album.

The third film shot in 1963 was also shot on location, *Viva Las Vegas*. In this, one of his best musicals and certainly his most successful, grossing 5.5 million in the U.S.A. alone, Elvis is a singing racing car driver trying to raise money to buy a new engine. On the side, he woos Ann-Margret. Every picturesque background within fifty miles of the Vegas strip was photographed, and Elvis sang several appealing songs, including a duet with Ann-Margret. It was an altogether enjoyable film.

Viva Las Vegas was followed by *Kissin' Cousins,* one of the worst Presley films. Produced by Sam Katzman, "King of the Quickies," who usually finished a film in eight to fifteen days, the movie had all the appearance of a hastily produced TV show rather than a feature film. The story was as flimsy as most, but offered the twist of having Elvis in a dual role, playing an Air Force officer trying to persuade a hillbilly family to allow a missile base on their land, and playing the part of his own blond hillbilly cousin. There were songs, flabby humor, Daisy Mae-type girls, and a chance to see what Elvis would look like if he didn't dye his hair ink-black.

Kissin' Cousins was completed in less than two-and-a-half weeks at a total cost of 1.3 million dollars, about a third of what the likes of *Blue Hawaii* had cost. It was released by MGM before the already completed *Viva Las Vegas*.

Elvis's performance was professional, but matter-of-fact. There was no rock 'n' roll in his movies now. It

Neal Mathews, Bill Black, Elvis Presley, Scotty Moore

Hugh Jarrett, Neil Matthews, Hoyt Hawkins, Elvis and Gordon Stoker

was obvious to anyone but the most devoted fan who listened to the albums, that Elvis was practically throwing the songs away as he sang them.

The recording sessions for the songs in his movies were now almost in a set pattern. The session began at nine in the evening, and eight hours later every one of the songs in the movie would be recorded. The excitement was gone from his singing. Anyone of his imitators could have done just as well and as predictably.

Elvis's first film in 1964 was *Roustabout,* which told a tale about cold-hearted business types moving in to shut down a fumbling carnival run by Barbara Stanwyck. The soundtrack was another million-record seller.

The next film made was *Girl Happy,* in which Elvis was cast as a night-club singer who finds love and reasons for singing eleven songs to Shelley Fabares in Fort Lauderdale during the Easter vacation. This film committed the scenic blunder of placing mountains in Florida. Otherwise it was pleasant enough, with Nita Talbot doing a strip-tease while covered with newspapers.

Elvis's third and last film for 1964 was *Tickle Me,* for Allied Artists. It had Elvis playing a singing rodeo rider who gets a job on an expensive dude ranch and health resort that caters almost exclusively to voluptuous girls who spend most of their time in peekaboo bathing suits. Elvis, when not exercising the girls, looks for buried treasure in a ghost town. *The New York Times* said of this film: "This is the silliest, feeblest and dullest vehicle for the Memphis Wonder in a long time."

Elvis's second film for Sam Katzman and his first "costume" film was *Harum Scarum* (originally called *Harum Holiday*). This musical adventure had Elvis running around some mythical Arab kingdom like a Rudolph Valentino sheik. He played an American movie star and singer who gets involved with the daughter of the local king, prevents a political assassination, romances and sings and finally ends up in Las Vegas entertaining everybody.

This film was shot in eighteen days. Elvis was paid a million dollars and was owed the usual 50% of the profits. With an arrangement like that, the quality of the film was the last thing on anyone's mind. Colonel Parker figured that if they made a film for less money, then he and Elvis would receive more of the profits.

The eighteen Presley films which have gone into release since his 1957 debut picture, *Love Me Tender,* have grossed an estimated $175,000,000 at the box office.

Frankie and Johnny, a film for United Artists, was another quickie film, shot in four and half weeks. It was a much reworked version of the original story that had Elvis, a riverboat gambler, romancing Donna Douglas. "Even compared to some previous Presley turkeys," wrote *The New York Times,* "this one almost sheds feathers from the start."

The next film released was *Paradise, Hawaiian Style,* a sort of remake of *Blue Hawaii,* in which Elvis played an airline pilot whose inordinate interest in girls gets him in trouble with his boss. To overcome this trouble Elvis convinces a buddy to

Andy Griffith, Steve Allen, Imogene Coca, Elvis

set up a charter helicopter service of their own. There was lovely scenery, lovely girls, songs and nothing much else. The soundtrack sold profitably.

In 1965, as Elvis was celebrating his thirtieth birthday, the number-one song in America was "I Feel Fine," the fifth consecutive number-one song for the Beatles. Their popularity even surpassed Elvis's golden years as the Number One Rock 'n' Roll Singer in the World. Later in the year, the Beatles visited Elvis in his Bel Air home, joining him in an impromptu jam session, and although the Beatles themselves said Elvis was what inspired them, Elvis didn't have any number-one songs from the spring of 1962 to the winter of 1969. Elvis was already a relic from the past, merely surviving and repeating himself in bland films and equally bland songs.

The pictures continued to appear, as regularly as the school holidays. In 1966 Elvis made *Spinout,* his second with Joe Pasternak and sixth with director Norman Taurog. This was another one about fast cars, girls and singing.

In *Double Trouble,* Elvis plays a tuxedoed rock 'n' roll singer who is supposed to be in love with two girls —an aggressive tease and a naive English heiress, while being followed by a trio of weird detectives, played by the Wiere Brothers.

The final film for 1966 was *Easy Come, Easy Go,* in which Elvis plays a Navy frogman searching for sunken treasure and a good time. This one had three songs and a cameo appearance by Elsa Lanchester.

And then, just before he married in the spring of 1967, Elvis appeared in *Clambake* as the son of an oil millionaire who wants to be loved for himself and not his money. So he exchanges places with a Florida ski instructor and winds up in a ski boat regatta, beating his rival in the film after singing seven songs.

Over the years, Elvis's name had been linked with those of perhaps a hundred girls—some well known, some not so well known, many of them his leading ladies. Almost all the relationships, no matter how superficial or innocent, were heavily publicized, either by the eager actress's press agent or the prying and exaggerating fan magazines.

Friends said Elvis enjoyed being a bachelor too much and he'd never give it up for marriage, surely not for several more years.

Elvis was married in Las Vegas on May 1, 1967, with only a few close friends attending, and, at the reception, one hundred members of the press.

The girl he married was Priscilla Beaulieu, whom he had dated, on and off, since he met her in West Germany, where she was living with her father, an Army colonel.

Elvis said he was thirty-two; Priscilla said she was twenty-one, both reported it was their first marriage.

It was too late to soothe all the hurt feelings caused when Priscilla came between Elvis and his buddies. Priscilla didn't care for some of them, and they didn't care for her. Only two of the old "Memphis Mafia" remained, one remaining as secretary-bookkeeper-confidant, while the other continued as Elvis's valet and began working more closely with Elvis in his films.

Elvis bought a new house in Southern California, reportedly for $400,000. Except for the change of address and marital status, everything else remained the same. The feeble film scripts that usually went like this: Elvis in boat; Elvis waving at girls; Elvis singing it up; Elvis hitting somebody; Elvis driving away; Elvis singing again—continued to pour in.

Elvis reported for work on *Speedway* in June. In this picture he plays a hotshot car driver, who, because of his manager's fondness for horse racing, owes the Internal Revenue Service a small fortune. The IRS sends an undercover agent, Nancy Sinatra, after Elvis and it looks like jail time for him, but Elvis wins the big race, pays Uncle Sam with the winnings and gets the girl. Of course Nancy and Elvis sang enough songs to fill up one side of an album.

Wrote *The New York Times:* "Music, youth and customs were much changed by Elvis Presley twelve years ago; from the twenty-six movies he has made since he sang "Heartbreak Hotel," you would never guess it!"

In September Elvis started *Stay Away, Joe,* the first film since *Wild in the Country* that didn't follow the routine Presley story line. Elvis plays a shabby Navajo Indian who cons a Congressman into giving him a herd of cows, which he sells; then he starts to chase the Indian maidens on the reservation. Elvis completed the picture in November, about the same time *Clambake* was released to the usual mixed reviews.

Nine months to the day after Elvis and Priscilla were wed, a child was born, weighing six pounds, fifteen ounces. They named her Lisa Marie.

Elvis's first film in 1968 was *Live a Little, Love a Little,* for MGM. This time he is a photographer with two bosses: the publisher of a *Playboy-*type magazine, and a high-fashion advertising executive. The *Live a Little, Love a Little* script included several "dammits" and had Elvis rising from a bed recently shared with Michele Carey, the shapely starlet who pursues him through most of the picture.

Not too many months before, an MGM executive was quoted as saying, "He (Elvis) has never made a dirty picture. They never go to bed in a Presley picture."

"I don't think I'm changing my image," Elvis said at the time. "I think you have to mature a little bit."

Elvis's image *was* changing, and in the next picture, *Charro,* filmed in the summer of 1968, he abandoned several more "trademarks." Usually in his films Elvis was given a nice wardrobe, but in this one, his third western, he wore the same grimy and dusty outfit throughout. He also appeared in the film unshaven, looking much like the former outlaw he was supposed to be. In the story, he is asked to find his old gang, then being sought for stealing a gold and bronze cannon that fired the last shot in the Mexican revolution. Not only was his face partially hidden in the scruffy beginnings of a beard, but his hair was covered by a hat. He didn't even smile, nor sing any song save one over the credits. As a western, it was too leisurely paced and not violent enough to be successful, and Elvis wasn't actor enough to carry it on mere characterization.

In the next picture, *The Trouble With Girls (and How to Get into It),* Elvis was the manager of a Chautauqua troupe that gets mixed up in the affairs of one of the towns it visits. Elvis didn't even appear in the film until halfway through it. He sang a few songs and looked comfortable in long, wide sideburns and an ice-cream-white suit and hat. Otherwise the movie was fairly dull.

Just as there were such easily recognizable commodities as "the Jerry Lewis film," "the beach party film," and recently, the "kung-fu film," there was something called the "Elvis Presley film." By the time *Blue Hawaii* appeared in 1962, they had become so individualized that they were a category unto themselves.

The plots were little more than thinly-veiled vehicles designed to carry Elvis into a recording studio to produce another album of songs. The philosophy seemed to be, "Don't say it if you can sing it." And when in doubt about plot development or dialogue—*sing!* Add plenty of girls with shapely legs and healthy bosoms and picture-postcard scenery to distract from the feeble story line, and you have an Elvis Presley film.

The supporting cast was composed of talented character actors and fading stars (Arthur O'Connell, Gig Young, Dolores Del Rio, Barbara Stanwyck) on one side and a steady stream of young people (Gary Lockwood, Bill Bixby, Shelley Fabares, Yvonne Craig) on the other. Plus lots of shiny land, sea and air vehicles. And, of course, the added ingredient of Elvis punching someone. In every film, Elvis slugs someone, sooner or later, and always for a good reason.

Essentially they were all fantasies, totally unrelated to reality, or to anything outside of Elvis's world.

Kissin' Cousins was the turning point in the filming of all future pictures. When the studios and the Colonel realized how fast they could make the films, Elvis and the shooting company were always on short schedules. There was seldom rehearsal for all the numbers.

Elvis always quit at six o'clock and usually rehearsed during his lunch hour. There would be six or seven songs in the film and there was never any time on the schedule for him to rehearse properly.

It started with the attitude of the studios he worked with. They never used Elvis to his full capacity in the situations in these films, nor in the songs that were given to him. The studio and the Colonel had the attitude—OK, here's the schedule, and because it's Elvis, we're going to make so much money that it doesn't matter much what he does or what he sings. Anything was good enough because Elvis was in it, and the fans would just eat it up no matter what. All the studio dreamed of was that each film would make two and half times its negative cost, and that meant a profit for everyone.

Directors usually handled Elvis with kid gloves. There was one picture that was thirty minutes late in starting, which is a lot of time when you're on location. They were late because Elvis wasn't there. And Elvis wasn't there because the director was afraid to send somebody to knock on his dressing room door. His best performances have been with gutsy directors like Michael Curtiz, but there haven't been very many of them.

Elvis with Shelley Faberes in "Girl Happy"

Many felt Elvis was talented; even the hard-to-please *New York Times* had said: "This boy can act," about his portrayal in *King Creole*. But that was a long time ago, before the weight of mindless, glossy films turned Elvis into a singing, dancing, romancing puppet. The gutsy vitality of Elvis's early songs and his exciting stage presence all but disappeared from his albums and films. He was more or less ignored or forgotten by the general pop scene, as the Beatles shook up the world with their music.

"I've had intellectuals tell me that I've got to progress as an actor," Elvis said in 1963, "explore new horizons, take on new challenges, all that routine. I'd like to progress, but I'm smart enough to realize that you can't bite off more than you can chew in this racket. You can't go beyond your limitations. They want me to try an artistic picture. That's fine. Maybe I can pull it off some day. But not now. I've done eleven pictures and they've all made money. A certain type of audience likes me. I entertain them with what I'm doing. I'd be a fool to tamper with that kind of success."

The Colonel once told a scriptwriter that there were a quarter of a million dyed-in-the-wool Elvis Presley fans who'd see every picture three times, that Elvis transcended any material he was assigned; when lines formed outside the theatres, those in the lines were there *to see Elvis and nothing else.*

This was beginning to change by 1966. Elvis had put on weight and his dyed hair was sprayed with so much lacquer you could bounce rocks off it. In an era of long, un-

washed hair, of the Beatles and hard and soft drugs, even loyal Presley fans stopped going to his films. One fan magazine called the films "animated puppet shows for not-so-bright children." Elvis began to wonder about the product he was turning out, first showing boredom and then occasional pique. Those present when Elvis cut songs for the movies said he wandered over after listening to one of the demonstration records and said, "What can you do with a piece of shit like that?"

Elvis Presley,
Laura Figueroa

But apparently Elvis never said anything to the Colonel. Elvis preferred to go along rather than fight with anyone. The years of having it easy and having it rich without much responsibility eroded any integrity he had as an artist. When asked why he kept making those rotten films, Elvis said he left all that to the Colonel.

While turning out cream-puff musicals, Elvis became the highest-paid entertainer in history. As the quality of the films went down, Elvis's earnings went up, up, until he began to average five and six million dollars a year. Other performers may have been wealthier, but none were paid so much for performing. He was getting a million dollars *plus* 50% of the profits, and for the better part of his career all the films were profitable.

"They don't need titles," said an MGM studio executive who worked on five of them. "They could be numbered. They would still sell."

Elvis also contracted to do more pictures per year than any other superstar. Other stars might insist on script approval and be picky about what they'd do, but Elvis would sing through anything he was given, and few pictures were so complicated that they required more than five or six weeks to shoot.

When Elvis and the Colonel celebrated their tenth anniversary together, the Colonel said the seventeen films released to date (April 1965) had grossed between 125 and 135 million dollars. Then, not to be outdone, RCA said Elvis had sold 100 million records valued at 150 million dollars.

Technical Advisor: Colonel Tom Parker

Every Elvis Presley film has the credit *Technical Advisor: Colonel Tom Parker*. Regardless of the sub-ject matter of the film, the Colonel is *the* Technical Advisor. Does the Colonel advise Elvis on how to drive a car, fly a plane, or sail a boat? Or does the Colonel advise Elvis on how to sing, dance and romance? No, it's nothing so trivial as that. The Colonel is the guiding hand that pulls all the strings on that singing-dancing-romancing puppet Elvis be-came. The Colonel's name on an El-vis Presley film is like a manufac-turer's trademark on a prepackaged product. And that product—Elvis Presley—is a worldwide, multimil-lion-dollar industry which has lasted almost twenty years.

Colonel Parker sold Elvis into bond-age, a princely and not too reluctant bondage, when Elvis was in his prime. Elvis was committed to mak-ing some of the worst movies any star ever made. For ten years he labored with bland songs, barely worth singing, clichéd plots and me-chanical performances, until the very mention of an Elvis Presley film brought laughter and snickering from all but the most dedicated fan. These movies were the visible docu-ment of Elvis's decay from the dy-namic power incarnate of rock 'n' roll to a mere singing-dancing-romancing puppet.

Many people blamed the Colonel exclusively for this, forgetting that Elvis must share an equal blame. He could have demanded better material, showed more independence. But Elvis, one of the two idols of the rebellious youth of the 1950s was, in his personal life and behavior, very docile to the wishes of his elders—Colonel Parker, the producers, the directors.

Once the Colonel saw what Elvis was and could be, he devoted all his skill to promoting Elvis. He was with him constantly until Elvis was totally under the hypnotic control of the Colonel's personality. The Colonel knew all about the care and feeding of a star. Under his managing, Elvis floated on a cloud of adoration. He never witnessed any pressure. He just had to appear, do his thing and depart. He was totally free, freer than any other star.

The Colonel kept Elvis "loose," so that subsequently Elvis would do anything he wanted him to do. Most artists have no inkling of how to operate a business; if the artist wants to be successful economically, he has to believe in a businessman as much as the businessman says he believes in the artist. The Colonel's business managing made Elvis very rich and

very comfortable. Consequently, Elvis seldom doubted or questioned the Colonel's wishes.

The Colonel's comfort campaign included having people next to Elvis who were the people he liked, and who could keep other people away. That is why the "Memphis Mafia" was close to him. Elvis had all the companionship he wanted, and he didn't need outsiders.

Whether Elvis would have been as big a star without the Colonel's maneuvering and managing is difficult to say. Both would have succeeded separately, but together they were a phenomenal success, far exceeding the wildest dreams of either.

The Colonel didn't just sell Elvis to the public. He sold Elvis to the people who sell the public—the media people, television and motion picture personalities, the important radio people. Elvis, as a product, is always in the state of being sold.

The Colonel communicated with these people regularly and he drew on their energies, pulling them along with him. He made it fun for them and that's why they went along. Each was made to feel he was contributing to the career of Elvis Presley.

A Different Kind of Role... A Different Kind of Man

Something happened in 1968 to change the Presley image more than any film could. It had been announced by the Colonel in January that NBC would finance and produce a one-hour special to be broadcast during the Christmas holidays and later would finance and produce a motion picture as well—a combination making it possible for the Colonel to keep the Presley salary near the million-dollar level. Elvis's films had been dropping in popularity and profits lately, and unless the Colonel agreed to do a film *and* a special, probably the million-dollar figure would not have been met anywhere in Hollywood. This initiated what afterwards was to be called Elvis's "comeback," or more precisely, his moment of truth.

If Elvis did another movie musical or the TV special, he could possibly wipe out his career and be known as that phenomenon who came along in the fifties, shook his hips and had a great manager. On the reverse side, if he could do a show that proved he still could galvanize the fans with his presence and performance, then his career would be in full swing again.

The Colonel wanted Elvis to come out, say, "Good evening, ladies and gentlemen," sing twenty-six Christmas songs, and say, "Merry Christmas and good night."

But the director of the TV special, Steven Binder, wanted something different, something that would show the real Elvis, something to capture the excitement of his earlier performances. Elvis overruled the Colonel's decision and opted for the director's vision.

The production numbers were taped first. And in some of them the supporting cast was monstrous, with dancers and singers all over the stage. In one number his name in lights formed a background twenty feet high. The TV special was beginning to look better than any of his last dozen movies.

On the day of the live videotaping, before a live audience, Elvis was not sure of himself; as a matter of fact, he was frightened. He sat in makeup, sweating. He said to one of his entourage, "I haven't been in front of those people in eight years. What am I gonna do if they don't like me? What if they laugh at me?"

Elvis had performed on movie sets where there were sometimes three or four hundred people, but that was different. Those people were working; they were paid to laugh and scream for the camera. But there were real live people in the audience now.

At the last minute the Colonel suggested the prettiest girls in the audience be moved close to the stage, even to sit on the edge of it. He was moving around the crowd like a carnival barker, picking the faces he wanted, saying, "Who here really loves Elvis?"

Elvis finally came out in a black leather suit, and when he reached for the hand mike, his hand was actually shaking. But then he started to sing and it was all over. He was the same old confident Elvis that could face 30,000 screaming females and not worry about getting out alive.

The songs came naturally and forcefully as Elvis moved across the stage singing: "Blue Suede Shoes," "Heartbreak Hotel," "Love Me Tender," His black leather suit was shining in the strong spotlights, sweat gleamed on his forehead. The audience was mesmerized by this dark figure who was Rock 'n' Roll Incarnate—some adolescent fertility god returned from the grave, or, at least, exile. The applause was genuine and deafening.

"After it was all over," Steve Binder, the director of the show, said, "Elvis asked me what I thought as far as the future was concerned. I said, 'Elvis, my real feeling is that I don't know if you'll do any great things you want to do. Maybe the bed had been made already, maybe this'll be just a little fresh air you'll experience for a month. Maybe you'll go back to making another twenty-five of those movies.' He said, 'No, no, I won't. I'm going to do things now!' "

The show was broadcast Tuesday night at nine o'clock, December 3, and swamped everyone. The same week, the soundtrack album was released. Both the special and the album were favorably received.

"There is something magical about watching a man who has lost himself find his way home," said Jon Landau in *Eye*. "He sang with the kind of power people no longer expect from rock 'n' roll singers. He moved his body with a lack of pretension and effort that must have made Jim Morrison green with envy."

"It wasn't the old Elvis, trading on the nostalgia of early rock and obso-lete Ed Sullivan censorship," said the *Record World,* "it was a modish performer, virile and humorous and vibrating with the nervousness of the times."

The New York Times wrote that Elvis "helped bring the pop world from illusion to reality," and called Elvis "charismatic."

Elvis's movie income was falling noticeably enough for the Colonel to consider some personal appearances. For the time that went into it, it was more profitable for him to appear in person than in movies. It took Elvis fifteen weeks to make a movie, on the average. If he appeared for ten weeks, one concert a week at $100,000 each, he could do much better than appearing in a film very few people wanted to see. Elvis had two more films to do, but they were keeping open the possibility of a concert tour in eight or nine months.

Already Elvis was making changes—becoming a father, taking somewhat more meatier and more adult movie roles, and returning to television. There was another noticeable shift in 1968 and that was in his recordings. There were several besides the soundtrack albums. He recorded "Guitar Man," "U.S. Male," "You'll Never Walk Alone," and his first million-selling single in more than three years—"If I Can Dream."

In January 1969 Elvis walked into a recording studio in Memphis for the first time since he left Sun Records, fourteen years earlier. He had laryngitis for four days. But with sessions beginning at eight at night and running till dawn, he still cut thirty-six

It was Elvis's most productive recording session.

The movie *Charro* was released in March and only a few critics seemed to believe Elvis's first nonmusical represented much of an improvement, even if the ad copy said, "A different kind of role, a different kind of man." His records fared a little better. He recorded "Memories," and "In the Ghetto," which was another million-plus seller.

Elvis started on his last "formula" film, something prophetically called *Change of Habit*, where he played a doctor working in the ghetto, falling in love with one of his new nurses, who, unknown to him, is a nun. Elvis sang three songs in the film and was sporting a new hair style, longer and bushier, and seemed more relaxed.

In early July, he began rehearsals for what was to be his first public appearance in over eight years.

"I got tired of singing to the guys I beat up in the motion pictures," Elvis said the night he opened in Las Vegas.

The Colonel began negotiating a contract with the International Hotel, a thirty-story hotel (1,519 rooms) in Las Vegas. Elvis began to rehearse for his opening, playing and singing more than a hundred songs, picking twenty or so that he would use as the core of the show.

When word got out, fans from all over the world called Las Vegas for reservations. The opening week was sold out and the rest of the month nearly so.

songs, enough material to fill two albums—*From Elvis in Memphis*, released in May, and half of the *Memphis/Vegas* set released in October.

The King Returns

Yvonne Lime, Elvis Presley

In 1969, a rock revival began in this country. The old idols of rock were being called back from oblivion—Dion, Ricky Nelson, Little Richard, Bill Haley, Fats Domino, Chuck Berry, Jerry Lee Lewis. Elvis had been getting some promising press as well, thanks to improved record material, the television special, and because of the renewed interest in rock 'n' roll.

The night Elvis opened at the Showroom Internationale, a huge multi-leveled restaurant at the International Hotel in Las Vegas, every one of the two thousand seats was occupied. The atmosphere was one of growing tension and expectation as the crowd waited for the legendary singer.

The audience sat through a comic's routine that drew a few laughs, and through the four Sweet Inspirations singing show tunes—all mere warm-ups for the Main Event.

Elvis stood in the wings, drumming his fingers nervously against his thighs. He had doubts about himself, he wasn't sure he could "cut it" anymore. He had been overexposed professionally the way very few other performers have been. Ten years of movies whose only merit was that they made money, and ten years of progressively blander songs had all but destroyed Elvis's credibility with all but the most fanatic fans. Elvis was also aware that many of those

coming to see him were doing so because they considered him some kind of freak—the slick-haired, swivel-hipped curio from the fifties. As during his first TV special, he wondered what he would do if they laughed at him.

The band began pounding out a rolling, thunderous, "Baby, I Don't Care" rhythm and without a word from the announcer, Elvis sauntered to center stage, grabbed the microphone from its stand, hit a pose from the fifties—legs braced, knees snapping almost imperceptibly—and before he could begin the show, he was greeted with a deafening roar. He looked. All two thousand people were on their feet pounding their palms and whistling, many of them standing on their chairs and screaming.

Finally the ovation subsided, the band picked up the beat and Elvis hit the pose again. It was as if the audience had cheated time, leaving the sixties for the fifties; once more they were high school kids and rock 'n' roll was just beginning, and the voice that launched a million shrieks was back from exile.

He sang a shortened version of "Blue Suede Shoes," lasting only a minute and half. Applause, and the second song, "I Got a Woman," and then almost as an afterthought, something he'd forgotten, he said, "Good evening, ladies and gentlemen."

The next song was "Love Me Tender," and this was for the fans. He spotted a pretty girl near the edge of the stage and knelt down and kissed her. He kissed a second, and a third, and a fourth, working his way along the stage, still singing.

And from that, right into a medley of his early hits—"Jailhouse Rock," "Don't Be Cruel," "Heartbreak Hotel," and "All Shook Up."

Then, mock serious, he said, "This is the only song I could think of that really expresses my feeling toward the audience."

He sang "Hound Dog."

The audience was reacting, creating and distributing energy in massive waves. Elvis in turn reacted to them. His voice was deeper, richer, gutsier, more sensual than it was in the years of the cream-puff films.

Elvis was wearing a modified karate suit, tied at the waist and slashed down the front, all black. With all that black, the black hair covering the tops of his ears, almost Beatle-length, and the lean features of his face, the moves, the legs braced, snapping, stretching, he was once again the whirling dervish of sex.

He closed with "What'd I Say," and two thousand people were on their feet. Elvis bowed and left, and came back to sing the song he intended to close with, the song he has since

closed every show with, "Can't Help Falling in Love."

The thunderous applause continued as Elvis moved through the good wishes and glad hands backstage, heading for his dressing room to change for the press conference the Colonel had arranged.

The critics were ecstatic. "Elvis Retains Touch in Return to Stage," *Billboard* headlined. *Rolling Stone* proclaimed: "Elvis was supernatural, his own resurrection." *Variety* called him a superstar, said he was "immediately affable . . . very much in command of the entire scene," while proving himself to be one of the most powerful acts in Vegas history. "There are several unbelievable things about Elvis," wrote *Newsweek,* "but the most incredible is his staying power in a world where meteoric careers fade like shooting stars."

At the end of the month-long run, two shows a night, seven nights a week, the hotel announced that Elvis had attracted 101,500 customers, far more than anyone else.

In December, Elvis's thirty-first movie, *Change of Habit,* was released. Because of the enthusiasm over his Vegas appearances and renewed interest on his recordings, the film was practically and kindly overlooked. Where it was noticed, it was criticized or laughed at, a ghost from Elvis's past.

Elvis Presley, Judy Tyler

When announced that Elvis would return to the International Hotel in January 1970, some said it was too soon, that he should have waited a year as suggested in the original contract. They said the winter engagement would only disappoint those who recalled so vividly his return from "retirement." To go back in only five months, and to do so during the slack season, would be a mistake. Of course, they were wrong. By mid-January, a week before opening, all but seven days of the twenty-nine had been sold out—nearly four thousand seats a night. Elvis had such a following, so many fans, that they flew in, checked in, and stayed a week or two, going to every show.

For his second appearance at Vegas, Elvis decided to shift the emphasis from his songs to songs made popular by other vocalists.

On opening night, January 26, Elvis stood on stage, wearing a white jump suit slashed to the sternum, fitted closely at the waist and knees and belted with a macrame belt. His high collar was dripping with semiprecious jewels. Even his fingers seemed encrusted with gold and diamonds, enough to ransom a king.

He began to sing "All Shook Up" and then "That's All Right, Mama." He then entered into "Proud Mary," "Walk a Mile in My Shoes," and his next million-seller, "Kentucky Rain."

He sang "Suspicious Minds" with a half dozen karate kicks and some amazing leg-stretching and several knee drops. Then he went into his regular closing song, "Can't Help Falling in Love." After which he dropped to one knee, holding one arm aloft in the classic gladiator poise.

Out front the entire audience was on its feet, wildly applauding, whistling and shouting. Their ebullience caused the crystal chandeliers in the ceiling to swing noticeably.

Elvis closed February 25, a day later than originally scheduled. A few days later he and the band flew to Houston, Texas to perform in the Astrodome. There he performed six times, being the featured attraction of the annual Houston Livestock Show and Rodeo.

Like the International Hotel, the Astrodome was a logical choice, in spite of the terrible acoustics of the baseball park. There were 44,500 comfortable seats, the temperature was a constant seventy-two, and a one-mile-an-hour breeze provided circulation, in the "eighth wonder of the world." Elvis was guaranteed $100,000 a show, plus a percentage of the box office. Performing three evening and three matinee shows, Elvis walked away with a reported 1.2 million dollars.

Another reason for appearing at the Astrodome was its location, for it

had been in East Texas that Elvis got one of his first big pushes in 1954 and 1955: it was here that the early fans had been thickest, and Elvis genuinely wanted to return to them. Another reason was the price of admission: tickets had been scaled down to a dollar, so even the poorer fan could get in.

"To maintain his image as 'King,' Presley needs 'super engagements'; by appearing in Las Vegas's biggest showroom and in the Astrodome, he had just that," said the Colonel.

It had been more than a year since Elvis finished his last film, *Change of Habit,* fulfilling all his commitments. Of course the Colonel had been made some offers during this period, but the terms dictated by him were enough to shatter any producer. The Colonel wanted a million dollars for ten weeks of Elvis's time, plus 50% of the profits; 25% of the television sale on top of the 10% for television distribution; total cost of picture not to exceed two million dollars; no shooting after six on weekends; no work the last two weeks in December and the first two in January; and if the picture isn't finished in ten weeks . . . tough luck!

The Colonel was a little leery of deflecting the growing popularity of Elvis by having him appear in another of those fluffy musicals, which nobody really wanted to see anymore. There was an almost subliminal hunger for the "real" Elvis to expose himself, after all those years of pretty, plastic poses.

The Colonel announced that Elvis would star in a documentary film about himself. It would be called *Elvis* and was to be shot in rehearsal and on stage at the International Hotel in August.

Filming had begun back in Los Angeles, as Elvis started rehearsals at an MGM rehearsal hall, and the documentary's Oscar-winning director, Denis Sanders, explained that about half the film—50 to 60 minutes —would be edited from Elvis's first five performances in the International Showroom; the rest would be scenes and interviews. Budget for the film was between one million and 1.3 million, little of which went to Elvis.

Denis Sanders came to the project with an astonishing background for an Elvis Presley director. He had worked in television documentary, directed segments of TV series and even two films. His *Czechoslovakia, 1968* won the Oscar for best documentary in 1969.

wasn't the freak out of the fifties, surviving on the fanatical devotion of his fans. He wasn't the has-been many people expected to see. Instead, he stood out in all his showbiz splendor, reacting to the audience with consummate skill, moving with more grace than he had ever displayed in his other films. Elvis was the most precise visual presentation of the word "superstar."

". . . Elvis is magnificent, more powerful than ever as he sings twenty-seven numbers, still one of the most compelling of all rock performers," wrote Henry S. Resnik in *Saturday Review*.

A few dissenting voices were heard: "If anything at all is revealed about the personal Elvis, it is that there is little to reveal about him. He is dynamite on stage, but a shallow, colorless, immature and insecure boy when he's off," wrote Gail Rock in *Women's Wear Daily*.

For over a decade, Elvis Presley had been so swathed in mystery, so cushioned by wealth, so enormous in reputation and so manipulated, visually and cinematically, it was almost impossible to believe in his existence. You saw him on film, you heard him on records, but did he *really* exist?

Millions of teenagers have screamed and fainted at his performances, but none of them actually knew anything about the person they were screaming at. Perhaps this mystery heightens his appeal. Each fan is able to create the image of his hero he or she prefers and the only demands on a spectator or fan is to pay attention to the actual performance.

On opening night at the International, Sanders took his forty-man crew, which included the famous cameraman Lucien Ballard, and eight Panavision cameras into the Showroom. Five of the cameras remained rolling throughout the hour-long show.

The result was a film that for the first time presented to moviegoers the real Elvis, or as close to the real one as it is possible to get. He appeared more interesting, more dynamic and human than in any of his previous plastic roles. He shone through as a rather nice, rather human, hard-working performer. He

The concerts continued to be sold out, as hundreds of thousands rushed to see and hear the living legend from out of the past. The avid Elvis fans were vindicated in their faith in him. The marginal Elvis fan returned to the fold, and many who only knew his name came to cheer and scream as he appeared.

There were rumors that his wife Priscilla had been discontented with life in a gilded cage, that she had been persuaded to put aside her own show-business ambitions "for Elvis." The marriage that was made in heaven was about to crash to earth.

In June 1972, Elvis gave three concerts in New York City, at Madison Square Garden. He was the only performer in American show-biz history ever to become the god of his decade without once having played in New York City, media capital of America.

The same women who as teenagers had once thronged the city to see his first movie open in Times Square were now waiting in line—some with their daughters—for tickets to see Elvis in the flesh.

At the Garden, the lights went down, the conductor raised his baton, and the small orchestra launched into the famous thunderous first notes of Strauss's *Also Sprach Zarathustra*—more popularly recognized as the theme from Kubrick's film, *2001: A Space Odyssey*.

Already the flashbulbs were popping like strobe lights. The audience was tense with excitement and anticipation. Suddenly Elvis materialized in a white suit of light, shining with golden appliqués, the shirt front slashed to show his chest. Around his shoulders was a cape, lined in cloth of gold, its collar faced with scarlet. He looked like the hero of some science-fiction comic strip—narrow-eyed, with high cheekbones, smooth, tanned skin and coal-black hair. He was girdled by a great golden belt with the legend "The World Champion Entertainer." When he started to work with the mike, his right hand flailing air, his left leg moving as though it had a life of its own, time stopped, and every one in the place was seventeen again. He radiated supreme self-confidence and that legendary animal magnetism.

Elvis sang a mixed bag of new and old songs, but it was when he got to the old Elvis numbers that the audience came unglued. Young girls moaned, and stood in their seats trying to dance.

Throughout, Elvis maintained a certain ironic distance from it all, sometimes engaging in a bit of self-parody. At the beginning of "Hound Dog" he posed dramatically on one knee, said, "Oh, excuse me," and switched to the other knee. He was still coming on strong with humor, and near-balletic pistoning body-work that both formalized and shrewdly mocked his image.

"It was bliss," a young woman in the audience said, "I haven't felt so intensely thirteen since—well, since I was thirteen."

Elvis gave a rare press conference in New York during his Garden show, where he drew 80,000 people and grossed $730,000. When asked how he was able to last longer than most pop performers, he answered with a half smile, "I guess it's because I take large doses of vitamin E."

Elvis at press conference

How did Elvis outlast all of the others in the pop-idol field? Mainly it was because he was more talented than any of them, possessing an extremely fine and individual voice and singing style. Secondly, Elvis had perhaps the shrewdest personal manager in all of show business. Thirdly, there is that strange performer-audience rapport that only the true superstars in any field of entertainment have. In addition, his personal inaccessibility made him an object of continuous interest. But more simply it was that Elvis Presley was unique, a one-of-a-kind item. He is one of those individuals whose presence and personality have etched themselves forever on the world's consciousness.

In July 1972, Elvis and his wife of five years separated, and on August 18, Elvis sued Priscilla for divorce, because, as his lawyer said, "Elvis has been spending six months a year on the road, which put a tremendous strain on the marriage." On October 19, 1973 the divorce decree was final, with Priscilla keeping the child and a handsome monthly allowance for alimony and support.

From the concert tour in 1972, another film documentary was produced by MGM, *Elvis on Tour,* released in 1973.

Elvis's second TV special was "Elvis: Aloha from Hawaii" which was aired over NBC in April 1973. The show consisted of eighteen songs, sixty minutes of which was a satellite concert presented earlier in January 1972 and delivered live to Australia, Japan, Korea, New Zealand, Thailand, South Vietnam and the Philippines, and, on January

15, to the twenty-eight nations in the Eurovision telecast system. That concert reached at least one and half billion viewers in the worldwide hookup. To that concert was added thirty minutes of specialty material, and that was the show broadcast as the NBC special. The show was rebroadcast in early 1974, both times gathering a large audience in the U.S.A.

As Elvis enters into his forties, the picture that emerges of this legendary star still borders on the fantastic. He is inaccessible to just about everyone except his "Memphis Mafia," a phalanx of bureaucrats and bodyguards that surround him as if he were the President of the United States. The security around him is as tight as any for the President. Elvis lives in fear of kidnapping—not so much his own abduction, but that of his only daughter. There have been rumors that he even travels with a bulletproof vest, but that could be only the midriff bulge that dieting cannot rid him of. The only contact with the outside world comes during his concerts. Elvis generally sleeps until late afternoon and almost never ventures out when he does awaken.

For recreation Elvis sings gospel songs with his cronies, may practice karate with the likes of Chuck Norris or Bill Wallace, both world champions, or watch one of the countless television sets that adorn almost every room of his mansion. He is still the most famous recluse since Howard Hughes.

The serpentine moves, the animal magnetism, the sideburns and hair are still there. The voice is less raunchy, more professional, but his lamé bodysuits paunch out in some different places. The lean, intense look is gone, Elvis is definitely beginning to be middle-aged. He fights the middle-age midriff bulge with extreme dieting and exercising, but it is a losing battle. Several times this dieting has lead him to physical exhaustion and Elvis has had to be hospitalized.

He hasn't appeared in a film in years, yet offers are always coming in. The most serious one was from Ray Stark, producer of Barbara Streisand's *Funny Girl* and *Funny Lady*. Both Stark and Streisand wanted Elvis to co-star in a musical remake of *A Star Is Born*. Had Elvis accepted the offer and the challenge of a serious film role, he could have initiated his film comeback, one that could have placed him on the Top Ten box-office list. But Elvis (or the Colonel) said no.

Elvis hasn't appeared in a formula film since 1969 *(Change of Habit)*. Seven years without a film is a long hiatus for the man who made three films a year for nearly ten years. Some say he is no longer interested in films, and will certainly never make another musical of the type he became infamous for. Others claim Elvis is waiting for the right ma-

terial for his cinematic comeback, something that will forever separate him from the "singing-dancing-romancing puppet" roles. With each passing year the odds seem to favor Elvis's *never* making another film. Of course there may be "documentaries" of his concerts, but a full-length feature seems out of the question.

It would be suicidal for Elvis or for any producer to attempt another typical Elvis Presley film. He must expand into mainstream films—drama, melodrama, comedy, adventure—anything but the ninety-minute commercials for his record albums that he made in the past. Elvis has the film presence and lacks only the proper handling to realize his potential as a genuine movie star.

Ann-Margret, one of Elvis's co-stars in his musicals, and a female facsimile of Elvis Presley, made the transition from "singing sex kitten" to a competent actress in a "serious film," *Carnal Knowledge,* and later in Ken Russell's rock musical, *Tommy.* Frank Sinatra is another example of a singer who turned actor, making the transition in the film *From Here to Eternity,* and turning in several solid performances over the years.

Elvis could also make the transition once he takes himself seriously as an actor. Early in his career he did want to make serious films, but greed and shortsightedness steered him to mindless fluff films that stunted his artistic maturity as a singer and actor.

But there is in Elvis a reluctance to overextend himself, to expose his ego to possible failure and rejection. Heralded as a living legend before he

was twenty-five years old, Elvis has, over the years, followed the dictum, "Once you're a legend, you don't have to prove yourself." He was perfectly happy to ride on the crest of his popularity and not scale new heights. "I'm still afraid to this day," he said, "that one morning I'll wake up and find out that everything was a dream and that we're all still back in a two-room shack in Tupelo with no hope of getting out from under the poverty."

At present, Elvis's career is more or less in a state of stagnation. He continues to appear three times a year in Las Vegas, and tours the country on concert dates. His shows are beginning to appear increasingly bland and predictable. It is almost like the cycle of his movie musicals all over again, the sameness of songs and performance only slightly relieved now and then.

Elvis's recording career is minimal, with no new records and only reissues of past successes on the market. The world's greatest rock 'n' roll singer is strangely silent.

This is in no way saying that his career is finished or beginning to decline. He can still do concert dates outside the U.S., which he has been reluctant to do. Across middle America, Elvis is worshipped with a fervor akin to fundamentalist fanaticism. Overseas, in Europe, the Far East, Australia, his popularity is at times even greater. He could tour the world for the next ten years and find welcoming crowds.

We can speculate endlessly on Elvis's future; the possibilities are legion: television, worldwide concert tours, closed-circuit TV specials, perhaps

films. There's even the possibility of Elvis's entering political life. In 1964, he was asked to run for office in Tennessee. If an actor can be governor of California, there is no reason why a singer cannot be governor of Tennessee.

But Elvis Presley is so obviously one of the phenomena of our time that he is beyond any kind of prediction, or even criticism. He can be observed, analyzed, his influence graphed, but in the end we can only marvel at his presence in an increasingly bland world.

The only certainty is that as long as Elvis wants to perform he will find an audience. And for a man like Elvis, life means performing.

The King's Fandom

It is impossible to be an idol without someone to idolize you. Without legions of enthusiastic fans to support him, Elvis might well have been just another singer with a meteoric rise to public acclaim and an equally fast decline, instead of the mystic figure he is. These are the fans who make it abundantly clear that the word *fan* is short for fanatic.

Fans sew the titles of Elvis's movies on their skirts and shirts, the names of the characters he played on their bedspreads. They repeatedly see his films, listen to his records.

They save their money for pilgrimages to Graceland and Tupelo, where they shoot dozens of rolls of film, mostly of the gates, the house and each other. They treasure each snapshot like a holy relic.

They collect anything they can get their hands on—taking leaves from Tupelo trees, grass from the Graceland lawn, napkins stained with *his* sweat.

They decorate entire rooms, creating Elvis environments; covering the walls of bedrooms completely. A teenage fan in California had a photograph of Elvis laminated in plastic so it wouldn't get wet when she took it into the shower. Another fan sleeps under hundreds of Elvis's photos and the record player never stops playing his songs.

Colonel Parker has cultivated the fandom, almost from the beginning, regarding them as money in the bank. He sends mimeographed letters, full of news of their idol's doings, to all the club presidents of the numerous Elvis Presley Fan Clubs. Whenever Elvis's fans gather in a convention, as they do in many parts of the world, the Colonel always sends a telegram.

There are thousands of fan clubs all over the world. Many clubs take their names from one of Elvis's films —The Blue Hawaiians (California), The Love Me Tender Elvis Presley Fan Club (Louisiana), Kissin' Cousins International Fan Club. Others use titles from his songs: "Hound Dog" Elvis Fan Club, the Stuck on You Forever Elvis Presley Fan Club (West Malaysia). Other variations are: Ready Teddy Elvis Presley Fan Club (Quebec), the Sound of Elvis Fan Club of Australasia, Forever Faithful Elvis Presley Fan Club (New Jersey), the For Ever for Elvis Fan Club (with branches in Miami, Memphis, Mexico City, Brazil), the International Elvis Presley Fan Club (Germany), and the Elvis Presley Fan Club of Great Britain and the Commonwealth.

This link between star and fan is a symbiotic relationship, mutually beneficial. From this vast, worldwide horde of fans Elvis draws his adulation, his wealth, and his reason for being. The fans live out a fantasy of identification for Elvis, vicariously sharing his life. Without Elvis, the fans could switch their allegiance to another and survive. But without the fans, Elvis would dwindle into nothingness. His great fame is sustained by the ever-present interest of his fans, not by the continuous acknowledgement of the general public, which is fickle, ever casting its favor on someone new.

As beneficial as they are, the fans are also partly the reason for Elvis's reluctance to expand his talents. In this closed-circuit relationship of star and fan, there is no need for the outside world. Why struggle with a new discipline when the old formula gives you everything you want? Elvis has reached a level of competence and has no desire to go forward. This is the great stagnation that keeps him a middle-aged rock 'n' roll idol and not a mature artist. Whether he ever leaves his cocoon and tries something new and daring, it is of secondary importance to the fans. As long as Elvis is Elvis, and performs, they are happy.

"I think being an Elvis fan is like being in love," an eager twenty-three-year-old girl said. "You can't explain *why* or *how* it happened, but that feeling is just there and unmistakable."

"I think Elvis is genuinely amazed by some of his fans," said a member of his entourage. "I've seen looks in his eyes that say, 'Man, you're weird.' I mean, how could he take it all seriously after all these years?"

Love Me Tender

20th Century-Fox

Credits

Produced by David Weisbart.
Directed by Robert D. Webb.
Screenplay by Robert Buckner.
Based on a Story by
  Maurice Geraghty.
Photographed by Leo Tover, A.S.C.
Music by Lionel Newman.
Art Direction by Lyle R. Wheeler
  and Maurice Ransford.
Special Photographic Effects by
  Ray Kellogg.
Technical Advisor:
  Colonel Tom Parker.
Photographed in CinemaScope.

Cast

Vance	Richard Egan
Cathy	Debra Paget
Clint	Elvis Presley
Siringo	Robert Middleton
Brett Reno	William Campbell
Mike Gavin	Neville Brand
The Mother	Mildred Dunnock
Major Kincaid	Bruce Bennett
Ray Reno	James Drury
Ed Galt	Russ Conway
Kelso	Ken Clark
Davis	Barry Coe

Synopsis

Elvis is the youngest of four brothers and the only one not in the Confederate Army. The three brothers, Richard Egan, William Campbell and James Drury, rob a Federal payroll at the closing days of the Civil War, and then head home.

The family reunion is marred, however, when Richard Egan learns his sweetheart, Debra Paget, married El-

Richard Egan, Elvis Presley

James Drury, Debra Paget, William Campbell,
Elvis Presley, Mildred Dunnock, Richard Egan

vis when everyone thought he was killed in the war. Deciding to leave home again, Egan plans to say farewell to Debra at a family picnic while Elvis entertains with a few songs.

U.S. Army Major Bruce Bennett arrives to arrest Egan and his brothers, who are taken to trial. Elvis plots with other members of Egan's gang to free them. But Egan decides to return the money and hope for a light sentence. The gang makes a raid, however, and frees the brothers.

At the farmhouse, Egan refuses to be a fugitive and still plans to return the money. When the farm is surrounded by a posse, Debra stuffs the money in her dress and escapes with Egan.

Neville Brand tells Elvis that Debra has run off with his brother and the money. Elvis pursues them and wounds Egan. But when Neville Brand plans to finish Egan off, Elvis defends him and is mortally wounded himself. As Elvis dies, he whispers that everything is all right now for everyone. Egan can return the money and have the girl.

Songs
"Love Me Tender," "Let Me Be," "Poor Boy," "We're Gonna Move."

Running time: 89 minutes
Release date: 11/16/56

Richard Egan, Debra Paget, Elvis Presley

Loving You
Paramount

Credits
Produced by Hal B. Wallis.
Directed by Hal Kanter.
Screenplay by Herbert Baker and
  Hal Kanter.
From a Story by Mary Agnes
  Thompson.
Photographed by Charles Lang, Jr.,
  A.S.C.
Edited by Howard Smith, A.C.E.
Special Photographic Effects by
  John P. Fulton, A.S.C.
Process Photography by Farciot
  Edouart, A.S.C.
Art Direction by Hal Pereira and
  Albert Nozaki.
Costumes by Edith Head.
Makeup by Wally Westmore.
Music Arranged and Conducted by
  Walter Scharf.
Vocal Accompaniment by The
  Jordanaires.
Assistant Director: James Rosen-
  berger.
Technical Advisor: Colonel Tom
  Parker.
Photographed in VistaVision and
  Technicolor.

Cast
Deke Rivers . . . . Elvis Presley
Glenda . . . . Lizabeth Scott
Tex Warner . . . . Wendell Corey
Susan Jessup . . . . Dolores Hart
Carl . . . . James Gleason
Tallman . . . . Ralph Dumke
Skeeter . . . . Paul Smith
Wayne . . . . Ken Becker
Daisy . . . . Jana Lund

Synopsis

Elvis is a young truckdriver who wows the crowd at a political rally where he has come to deliver beer, but remains to sing a hot number with the band at the urging of press agent Lizabeth Scott and Wendell Corey, leader of the band. They persuade Elvis to join the band and they make the rounds of small-town appearances, with Elvis's popularity increasing with every stopover.

Lizabeth Scott gets Elvis to sign a personal contract for her to represent him, without Wendell Corey's knowing about it. Though Elvis is deeply interested in Dolores Hart, the band's girl singer, he becomes greatly attracted to Lizabeth Scott whose publicity gimmicks soon make him a celebrity. His build-up leads to a booking at a big theatre.

Elvis Presley, Lizabeth Scott, Jana Lund

Elvis Presley, Dolores Hart

James Gleason, a booking agent, plans a one-man concert for Elvis in a Dallas suburb, and for a publicity stunt, Lizabeth Scott buys Elvis a red and white convertible, pretending that it's an anonymous gift from an oil-rich widow. To pay for the car the band has to cut expenses and Dolores Hart is fired. To console her, Elvis drives Dolores to her farm home, where he enjoys the simple farm life with her family.

Lizabeth comes to Elvis and brings him back to town. When Elvis learns that Lizabeth is Wendell's ex-wife, he leaves and has a crackup in his old car. Lizabeth finds him unharmed and brings him back for the concert.

With Dolores besides him, Elvis accepts a big TV contract and asks Wendell and Lizabeth, who plan to remarry, to represent him.

Songs

"Let Me Be Your Teddy Bear," "Got a Lot of Livin' to Do," "Loving You," "Lonesome Cowboy," "Hot Dog," "Mean Woman Blues," "Let's Have A Party."

Running time: 101 minutes
Release date: 7/9/57

Elvis Presley, Dolores Hart

Wendell Corey, Elvis Presley, Lizabeth Scott

Jailhouse Rock

Metro-Goldwyn-Mayer

Credits

Produced by Pandro S. Berman.
Directed by Richard Thorpe.
Screenplay by Guy Trosper.
Based on a Story by Ned Young.
Photographed by Robert Bronner, A.S.C.
Edited by Ralph E. Winters.
Assistant Producer: Kathryn Hereford.
Music Supervised by Jeff Alexander.
Songs mostly by Mike Stoller and Jerry Leiber.
Additional songs by Roy C. Bennett, Aaron Schroeder, Abner Silver, Sid Tepper and Ben Weisman.
Art Direction by William A. Horning and Randell Duell.
Makeup by William Tuttle.
Special Effects by A. Arnold Gillespie.
Assistant Director: Robert E. Relyen.

Technical Advisor: Colonel Tom Parker.
Photographed in CinemaScope.
Sound by Perspecta Sound.

Judy Tyler, Elvis Presley

Elvis Presley, Judy Tyler

Cast

Vince Everett .... Elvis Presley
Peggy Van Alden ..... Judy Tyler
Hunk Houghton . Mickey Shaughnessy
Sherry Wilson .... Jennifer Holden
Eddy Talbot .... Dean Jones
Laury Jackson ..... Anne Neyland
Warden .... Hugh Sanders

Synopsis

Elvis is sent to the state prison after he accidentally kills a man in a bar-room fight. His cellmate, Mickey Shaughnessy, a former folk singer, is impressed by Elvis's singing talent on a television show from the prison and signs him to a contract as part-ners for a double act to follow their release.

Released ahead of Mickey, Elvis's first effort at singing in a small bar meets with failure, but he arouses the interest of Judy Tyler, an exploi-tation girl for Geneva Records. Judy arranges for Elvis to tape-record a song, and a new singing style is born. After initial rebuffs and discourage-ment, they form their own record company. Dean Jones, a disc jockey, gives their first record a "break" on his show and Elvis soon finds him-self a teenage idol.

Hugh Sanders, Elvis Presley

Elvis Presley, Mickey Shaughnessy

Success blinds Elvis to Judy's love for him and their relationship settles on a business partnership basis. As Elvis is about to star on a big television show, Mickey arrives and demands to take his place as partner on the show, but Mickey proves a flop. Throwing out their old contract, Elvis keeps Mickey on as a flunky.

Hollywood soon beckons and the breach between Judy widens when Elvis falls for his leading lady and decides to sell the record company. An argument with Mickey results, in which the latter strikes Elvis in the throat, resulting in the loss of his voice. Supported by Judy's love and Mickey's contrition, Elvis recovers and is ready to sing again, a wiser and better man.

Songs

"Jailhouse Rock," "Treat Me Nice," "Young and Beautiful," "I Wanna Be Free," "Don't Leave Me Now," "Baby, I Don't Care," "One More Day."

Running time: 96 minutes
Release date: 10/21/57

Elvis Presley, Mickey Shaughnessy

King Creole

Paramount

Credits

Produced by Hal B. Wallis.
Directed by Michael Curtiz.
Associate Producer: Paul Nathan.
Screenplay by Herbert Baker and
    Michael Vincente Gazzo.
Based on the Novel *A Stone for
    Danny Fisher* by Harold Robbins.
Photographed by Russell Harlan,
    A.S.C.
Edited by Warren Low, A.C.E.
Art Direction by Hal Pereira and
    Joseph MacMillan Johnson.
Special Photographic Effects by
    John P. Fulton, A.S.C.
Process Photography by Farciot
    Edouart, A.S.C.
Costumes by Edith Head.
Makeup by Wally Westmore.
Musical Numbers Staged by
    Charles O'Curran.
Music Adapted and Scored by
    Walter Scharf.
Vocal Accompaniment by The
    Jordanaires.
Assistant Director: D. Michael
    Moore.
Technical Advisor: Colonel Tom
    Parker.

Cast

Danny Fisher . . . . Elvis Presley
Ronnie . . . . Carolyn Jones
Nellie . . . . Dolores Hart
Mr. Fisher . . . . Dean Jagger
"Forty" Nina . Liliane Montevecchi
Maxie Fields . . . . Walter Matthau
Mimi . . . . Jan Shepard
Charlie LeGrand . . . . Paul Stewart
Shark . . . . Vic Morrow

Elvis Presley, Dolores Hart

Elvis Presley, Carolyn Jones

Elvis Presley, Walter Matthau, Carolyn Jones

Elvis Presley, Dean Jagger

114

Synopsis

Elvis works as a busboy at the Blue Shade, a cheap nightclub on Bourbon Street in New Orleans' French Quarter. There is an all-night drinking party still in progress, and after being forced to sing a song, Elvis rescues Carolyn Jones from a pawing hoodlum. Carolyn, property of racketeer Walter Matthau, wants to break away but doesn't dare.

Elvis, late for school, gets into a fight with classmates who see Carolyn kiss him goodbye, is told by the principal that he will not graduate. In an alley outside he is jumped by young hoodlums led by Vic Morrow, brother of the boy Elvis beat up. Despite the odds, Elvis wins the fight, and the young thugs invite him to join their gang. Elvis refuses.

Back home, Elvis's father, Dean Jagger, announces he has a new job in a drugstore, and begs the boy to go back to school full time, but Elvis refuses. Instead, he joins the young thugs led by Vic Morrow, acting as a decoy by singing while they rob a five-and-dime store. Before leaving, Elvis makes a date with Dolores Hart, who works there.

That night, Elvis is working at the Blue Shade when Carolyn walks in with Walter Matthau. Elvis greets her, but to allay Walter's suspicions she pretends she doesn't know him, and says she heard him sing only once. Walter Matthau challenges Elvis to sing, which he does, and is promptly offered a singing job by Paul Stewart, owner of the King Creole nightclub.

Elvis defies his father and accepts the job at the club, where he is a big hit nightly. Though he dates the

Elvis Presley, Dolores Hart

Dolores Hart, Elvis Presley

Elvis Presley, Walter Matthau

marriage-minded Dolores Hart, he and Carolyn have a strong attraction to each other, but she fears Walter too much to give in to it. Walter brazenly uses Carolyn to get Elvis to quit the King Creole and go to work for him, but Carolyn tips off Elvis and begs him not to get involved with Walter. When Elvis refuses to sing for Walter, the racketeer calls in Vic Morrow and orders him to get something big on Elvis. The "something big" involves a hold-up implicating Elvis and landing his father in the hospital.

In a rage Elvis gives Walter a terrible beating, which sets every hood in town on his trail. After a showdown fight with Vic Morrow, Elvis is taken to a country hideout by Carolyn and nursed back to health. But Walter tracks them down, kills Carolyn and is himself killed by one of his own gunmen, whom Elvis had befriended. Elvis returns to the King Creole, to Dolores Hart and his family.

Songs

"King Creole," "As Long As I Have You," "Hard Headed Woman," "Trouble," "Dixieland Rock," "Don't Ask Me Why," "Lover Doll," "Crawfish," "Young Dreams," "Steadfast, Loyal and True," "New Orleans," "Turtles, Berries and Gumbo," "Banana."

Running time: 115 minutes
Release date: 6/4/58

"A surprising colorful and lively drama, with Elvis Presley doing some surprisingly credible acting flanked by a dandy supporting cast ... Presley's third movie is generally a pleasure."

—Howard Thompson
The New York Times

G.I. Blues

Paramount

Sigrid Maier, Leticia Roman, Elvis Presley, Juliet Prowse

Juliet Prowse, Elvis Presley

Credits

Produced by Hal B. Wallis.
Directed by Norman Taurog.
Associate Producer: Paul Nathan.
Written by Edmund Beloin and
  Henry Garson.
Photographed by Loyal Griggs,
  A.S.C.
Edited by Warren Low, A.C.E.
Music Scored and Conducted by
  Joseph L. Lilley.
Musical Numbers Staged by
  Charles O'Curran.
Art Direction by Hal Pereira and
  Walter Tyler.
Costumes by Edith Head.
Special Photographic Effects by
  John P. Fulton, A.S.C.
Process Photography by Farciot
  Edouart, A.S.C.
Makeup by Wally Westmore.
Vocal Accompaniment by The
  Jordanaires.
Second Unit and Assistant Director:
  D. Michael Moore.
Military Technical Advisor: Captain
  David S. Parkhurst.
Technical Advisor: Colonel Tom
  Parker.
Color by Technicolor.

Cast

Tulsa McCauley . . . . . Elvis Presley
Rick . . . . James Douglas
Cooky . . . . Robert Ivers
Lili . . . . Juliet Prowse
Tina . . . . Leticia Roman
Marla . . . . Sigrid Maier
Sgt. McGraw . . . . . . Arch Johnson

Synopsis

Elvis and his two buddies, Robert Ivers and James Douglas, have formed a musical combo to fill the off-hours of their Army tour of duty in West Germany, hoping to save enough money to open a small night-club on their return to civilian life.

When a G.I. is suddenly transferred to Alaska on the eve of a campaign to win a $300 wager for himself and his buddies by spending the night with Juliet Prowse, a cabaret dancer with a heart of ice, Elvis is drafted to replace the departed G.I.

In a sincere effort to help his friends, and to win the wager, Elvis puts so much heart in his wooing that he falls in love with Juliet. As Elvis shows her the sights, Juliet realizes that they are being watched by Elvis's buddies to see that he lives up to the terms of the wager.

About this time, Elvis is drafted into service as a babysitter for the new son of his buddy James Douglas, who has gone off to get married. Elvis has problems with the baby and phones Juliet, who tells him to bring the child to her apartment.

And so, under very innocent circumstances, Elvis spends the night at Juliet's apartment. His buddies, who have been stationed outside the house, rejoice in the belief that he has lived up to the terms of the wager.

The following day, rehearsals are under way for a giant Armed Forces show. Elvis's sergeant is bragging of Elvis's success, and Juliet hears that she was only a military objective, that Elvis has played with her affections.

When James Douglas and Sigrid Maier, the baby's parents tell Juliet that Elvis was really doing them a favor in babysitting for them. Juliet realizes her mistake and her love for Elvis. They plan to marry, after the Army show.

Songs

"G.I. Blues," "Tonight Is So Right for Love," "Frankfurt Special," "Wooden Heart," "Pocketful of Rainbows," "Didya Ever?" "What's She Really Like?" "Shoppin' Around," "Big Boots," "Doin' the Best I Can."

Running time: 104 minutes
Release date: 10/20/60

Juliet Prowse, Elvis Presley

Elvis Presley, James Douglas, Robert Ivers, Arch Johnson

Elvis with children

Flaming Star

20th Century-Fox

Credits

Produced by David Weisbart.
Directed by Don Siegel.
Screenplay by Clair Huffaker and
　　Nunnally Johnson.
Photographed by Charles G. Clarke,
　　A.S.C.
Edited by Hugh S. Fowler.
Art Direction by Duncan Cramer
　　and Walter M. Simonds.
Music by Cyril Mockridge.
Musical Director: Lionel Newman.
Photographed in CinemaScope and
　　DeLuxe Color.

Cast

Pacer Burton . . . . Elvis Presley
Clint Burton . . . . Steve Forrest
Roslyn Pierce . . . . . . Barbara Eden
Neddy Burton . . . . Dolores Del Rio
Pa Burton . . . . John McIntyre
Buffalo Horn . . . . . Rudolfo Acosta
Doc Phillips . . . . Ford Rainey
Dred Phillips . . . . Karl Swenson
Angus Pierce . . . . . Richard Jaeckel
Dorothy Howard . . . . Anne Benton
Tom Howard . . . . L. Q. Jones
Will Howard . . . . . . Douglas Dick
Jute . . . . Tom Reese

Elvis and Dolores Del Rio

122

Synopsis

When a neighboring family is massacred by Kiowa Indians, the people of the town turn against Elvis and his family, demanding that they make it clear whose side they are on, the townspeople's or the Indians'. Elvis is half-Indian and his mother Dolores Del Rio is full Indian. His father, John McIntyre, says that they simply want to live in peace. The townspeople and the Indians will not accept their decision.

When a survivor of the initial massacre shoots Dolores Del Rio, Elvis joins the Indians. When a war party kills McIntyre, Steve Forrest then decides to fight the Indians single-handed. At night he attacks, killing the chief and several others, but receives almost fatal wounds himself. Elvis deserts the Indians to save his brother, ties him to his horse, sends him to town, and then turns to battle the pursuing Kiowas.

When Forrest wakes up in town, the girl who has sympathized with him, Barbara Eden, tries to keep him in bed, but he struggles to get up and goes to help Elvis. As he walks into the street, Elvis, near death, arrives on horseback to tell him that he is going to the mountains to die an Indian because he has seen the flaming star of death. Forrest watches helplessly as Elvis rides off.

Song

"Flaming Star."

Running time: 101 minutes
Release date: 12/20/60

"His (Presley's) is a dramatic performance—and a singularly effective one . . . It is the depth of feeling he reveals that comes as such a surprise."

—Arthur Knight,
Saturday Review

Elvis and Dolores Del Rio

John McIntyre, Elvis Presley

Wild in the Country

20th Century-Fox

Credits

Produced by Jerry Wald.

Directed by Philip Dunne.

Screenplay by Clifford Odets.

Based on a Novel by J. R. Salamanca.

Photographed by William C. Mellor, A.S.C.

Edited by Dorothy Spencer.

Associate Producer: Peter Nelson.

Music by Kenyon Hopkins.

Art Direction by Jack Martin Smith and Preston Ames.

Makeup by Ben Nye.

Costumes by Don Feld.

Song "Wild in the Country" by Hugo Peretti, Luigi Creatore and George Weiss.

Technical Advisor: Colonel Tom Parker.

Photographed in CinemaScope and DeLuxe Color.

Millie Perkins, Elvis Presley

Hope Lange, Elvis Presley

Tuesday Weld, Elvis Presley

Cast

Glenn Tyler . . . . Elvis Presley
Irene Sperry . . . . Hope Lange
Noreen . . . . Tuesday Weld
Betty Lee . . . . Millie Perkins
Davis . . . . Rafer Johnson
Phil Macy . . . . John Ireland
Cliff Macy . . . . Gary Lockwood
Uncle Rolfe . . . . William Mims
Dr. Underwood . Raymond Greenleaf
Monica George . Christina Crawford
Flossie . . . . Robin Raymond
Mrs. Parsons . . . . . . Doreen Lang
Mr. Parsons . . . . Charles Arnt
Sarah . . . . Ruby Goodwin
Willie Dace . . . . Will Corry
Professor Larson . . . . Alan Napier
Judge Parker . . . Jason Robards, Sr.
Bartender . . . . Harry Carter
Sam Tyler . . . . Harry Sherman
Hank Tyler . . . . Bobby West

Synopsis

Elvis is a rural boy of limited education and a discouraging environment who is branded a delinquent because of his rebellious attitude and antisocial behavior. Hope Lange is a psychiatric consultant who takes upon herself the task of rehabilitating the rebellious Elvis. She hopes to overcome his hostility and encourage his genuine talent for writing. She finds that her own interests are becoming more than just professional as she realizes that she is falling in love with Elvis. Tuesday Weld is the country girl who hinders Elvis's rehabilitation through her constant advances and urgings toward delinquency. Millie Perkins is Elvis's childhood sweetheart who places his future above her own needs, urging him to go to college and give her up, if necessary.

Hope Lange, Elvis Presley

Songs

"Lonely Man," "I Slipped, I Stumbled, I Fell," "In My Way," "Wild in the Country."

Running time: 114 minutes
Release date: 6/15/61

"Wild in the Country has something to recommend—mostly Elvis Presley and Hope Lange, both of whom at certain points demonstrate a flair for convincing expressions that overcome the generally slow pacing of the picture."

—Paul V. Beckley,
New York Herald Tribune

Blue Hawaii

Paramount

Credits

Produced by Hal B. Wallis.
Directed by Norman Taurog.
Associate Producer: Paul Nathan.
Screenplay by Hal Kanter.
Story by Allan Weiss.

Photographed by Charles Lang, Jr., A.S.C.
Edited by Warren Low and Terry Morse, A.C.E.
Special Photographic Effects by John P. Fulton, A.S.C.
Process Photography by Farciot Edouart, A.S.C.
Music Scored and Conducted by Joseph L. Lilley.
Musical Numbers Staged by Charles O'Curran.
Vocal Accompaniments by The Jordanaires.
Art Direction by Hal Pereira and Walter Tyler.
Costumes by Edith Head.
Makeup by Wally Westmore.
Technical Advisor: Colonel Tom Parker.
Photographed in Panavision and Technicolor.

Cast

Chad Gates . . . . Elvis Presley
Maile Duval . . . . . . Joan Blackman
Abigail Prentace . . . Nancy Walters
Fred Gates . . . . Roland Winters
Sarah Lee Gates . Angela Lansbury
Jack Kelman . . . . John Archer
Mr. Chapman . . . Howard McNear
Mrs. Manaka . . . . Flora Hayes
Mr. Duval . . . . Gregory Gay
Mr. Garvey . . . . Steve Brodie
Mrs. Garvey . . . . Iris Adrian
Patsy . . . . Darlene Tomkins
Sandy . . . . Pamela Alkert
Beverly . . . . Christian Kay
Ellie . . . . Jenny Maxwell
Ito O'Hara . . . . Frank Atienza
Carl . . . . Lani Kai
Ernie . . . . Jose De Varga
Wes . . . . Ralph Hanalie

Joan Blackman, Elvis Presley

Joan Blackman, Elvis Presley

Roland Winters, Angela Lansbury, Elvis Presley

Synopsis

Elvis returns to Hawaii after two years in the Army, determined not to do what his mother wants, which is to take a job in the family pineapple business, settle down and marry a girl of his own social position.

Instead Elvis gets a job as a guide in a tourist agency where his sweetheart, Joan Blackman, works, and his first assignment is escorting around the island four pretty schoolgirls, chaperoned by Nancy Walters.

One of the schoolgirls, Jenny Maxwell, develops a crush for Elvis and continuously throws herself at him, causing Elvis some trouble with his sweetheart.

Everything is resolved in the end, when Elvis marries Joan in a colorful boat wedding and they soon hope to open their own travel agency.

Songs

"Blue Hawaii," "Almost Always True," "Aloha Oe," "No More," "Can't Help Falling in Love," "Rock-a-Hula Baby," "Moonlight Swim," "Ku-u-i-po," "Ito Eats," "Slicin' Sand," "Hawaiian Sunset," "Beach Boy Blues," "Island of Love," "Hawaiian Wedding Song," "Stepping Out of Line."

Running time: 101 minutes
Release date: 11/14/61

Pamela Akert, Darlene Tompkins, Joan Blackman,
Elvis Presley, Jenny Marshal, Christian Kay

Follow That Dream

United Artists

Arthur O'Connell, Elvis Presley, Anne Helm

Anne Helm, Joanna Moore, Elvis Presley

Credits

Produced by David Weisbart.
Directed by Gordon Douglas.
Screenplay by Charles Lederer.
Based on the play, *Pioneer, Go Home!* by Richard Powell.
Photographed by Leo Tover, A.S.C.
Edited by William B. Murphy, A.C.E.
Music by Hans J. Salter.
Music Editor: Robert Tracy.
Technical Advisor: Colonel Tom Parker.
Photographed in Panavision and DeLuxe Color.

Cast

Toby Kwimper . . . . . . Elvis Presley
Pop Kwimper . . . Arthur O'Connell
Holly Jones . . . . Anne Helm
Alicia Claypoole . . . Joanna Moore
Carmine . . . . Jack Kruschen
Nick . . . . Simon Oakland
Eddy and Teddy Bascomb
             Gavin and Robert Koon
Ariadne . . . . Pam Ogles

Synopsis

Elvis and his father Arthur O'Connell have adopted, unofficially, three children and pretty Anne Helm, who is in love with Elvis.

Travelling through a southern state, they run out of gas and homestead on an unopened stretch of highway. Claiming squatter's rights, they settle and open a small business renting rowboats, fishing poles and bait and attract other homesteaders to the area. As the homesite is out of municipal and county jurisdiction, a couple of gangsters, Simon Oakland and Jack Kruschen, move a gambling trailer there and attract crowds and noise.

Anne Helm, Elvis Presley

Elvis is elected sheriff by the homesteaders and the gangsters hire hoods to beat up Elvis. Using judo, Elvis routs the hoods and clears the gangsters out. Meanwhile, Joanna Moore, State Welfare Superintendent investigates the "family" and proceeds to seize the children on the grounds of "bad moral climate." In a courtroom scene Arthur O'Connell and Elvis plead their case and the judge dismisses any legal charges.

Songs
"What a Wonderful Life," "I'm Not the Marrying Kind," "Sound Advice," "Follow That Dream."

Running time: 110 minutes
Release date: 3/29/62

Anne Helm, Elvis Presley

Kid Galahad

United Artists

Credits

Produced by David Weisbart.
Directed by Phil Karlson.
Screenplay by William Fay.
Based on a Story by Francis Wallace.
Photographed by Burnett Guffey,
    A.S.C.
Edited by Stuart Gilmore.
Art Direction by Cary Odell.
Music by Jeff Alexander.
Technical Advisor: Colonel Tom
    Parker.
Presented by The Mirisch Company.
Color by DeLuxe.

Cast

Walter Gulick . . . . Elvis Presley
Willy Grogan . . . . Gig Young
Dolly Fletcher . . . . . . Lola Albright
Rose Grogan . . . . . Joan Blackman
Lew Nyack . . . . . . Charles Bronson
Lieberman . . . . Ned Glass
Maynard . . . . Robert Emhardt
Otto Danzig . . . . David Lewis
Joie Shakes . . . . Michael Dante
Zimmerman . . . . Judson Pratt
Sperling . . . . George Mitchell
Marvin . . . . Richard Devon

Synopsis

Elvis is a sparring partner at a fighters' training camp owned by Gig Young. Elvis is not a good boxer, but he can absorb a lot of punishment and has a powerful right hand with which he knocks out Michael Dante, a professional boxer. Young immediately sees a fortune in Elvis and he sorely needs money to pay off a gambling debt to David Lewis, a gangster.

Elvis Presley, Joan Blackman

Elvis Presley, Joan Blackman

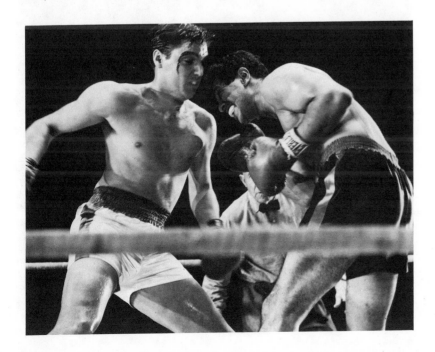

Young's sister, Joan Blackman, arrives to stay at the camp and falls for Elvis. After several fights, all KO's, Elvis proposes to Joan and they plan to marry as soon as he can quit the ring and go into business with a local garage owner. Young, however, is violently opposed to their romance.

When Lewis overmatches Elvis with one of his own fighters, far out of Elvis's class, Young's girl, Lola Albright, accuses him of overmatching Elvis for spite and leaves him. On the eve of the fight, Lewis offers Charles Bronson money for not working in Elvis's corner, because he wants to put his own "cut-man" there to make sure Elvis's cuts stay open. Bronson refuses and the hoods break his fingers. Arriving before the hoods leave, Young attacks them and is joined in a free-for-all by Elvis.

The night of the fight, Elvis KO's his opponent and his dressing room is the scene of happy confusion. Elvis will marry Joan; Young and Albright will be married too.

Songs

"King of the Whole Wide World," "This Is Living," "Riding the Rainbow," "Home Is Where the Heart Is," "I Got Lucky," "A Whistling Tune."

Running time: 95 minutes
Release date: 7/25/62

Girls! Girls! Girls!

Paramount

Credits

Produced by Hal Wallis.
Associate Producer: Paul Nathan.
Directed by Norman Taurog.
Screenplay by Edward Anhalt and Allan Weiss.
Story by Allan Weiss.
Photographed by Loyal Griggs.
Art Direction by Hal Pereira and Walter Tyler.
Music by Joe Lilley.
Musical Numbers Staged by Charles Curran.
Assistant Director: Mickey Moore.
Technical Advisor: Colonel Tom Parker.
Photographed in Panavision and Technicolor.

Cast

Ross Carpenter . . . . . . Elvis Presley
Robin Ganter . . . . . . Stella Stevens
Laurel Dodge . . . . Laurel Goodwin
Wesley Johnson . . . . . Jeremy Slate
Chen Yung . . . . Guy Lee
Kin Yung . . . . Benson Fong
Madame Yung . . . . Beulah Quo
Sam . . . . Robert Strauss
Alexander Starvos . . . Frank Puglia
Madame Starvos . . . . . Lili Valenty
Leona and Linda Starvos
        Barbara and Betty Beall
Arthur Morgan . . . . . . Nestor Paiva
Mrs. Morgan . . . . Ann McCrea
Mai and Tai Ling
        Ginny and Elizabeth Tiu

Synopsis

Elvis is a carefree but poor charter boat pilot who loses his boat when its owner sells it for medical ex-

Stella Stevens, Robert Strauss, Elvis Presley

Laurel Goodwin, Elvis Presley

penses. Elvis decides to buy his late father's sailboat, *"The West Wind,"* from Jeremy Slate. Being short of cash, Elvis starts singing at the local nightclub owned by Robert Strauss. In the daytime Elvis works for Jeremy Slate's tuna fleet.

At the nightclub Elvis meets wealthy Laurel Goodwin, who came to the seashore to forget a broken romance and falls for Elvis. She poses as a working girl and secretly buys the sailboat for Elvis. When Elvis finds out about the purchase his pride is hurt and he goes off to sulk. Laurel follows in a boat piloted by Jeremy Slate, who tries some hanky-panky with her. Elvis hears of this and rushes to the rescue, knocking down the sea wolf with a few punches. Elvis forces Laurel to sell the sailboat and decides to build a new boat, after marrying Laurel.

Songs

"Girls! Girls! Girls!" "I Don't Wanna Be Tied," "Where Do You Come From," "I Don't Want To," "We'll Be Together," "A Boy Like Me, A Girl Like You," "Earth Boy," "Return to Sender," "Thanks to the Rolling Sea," "Song of the Shrimp," "The Walls Have Ears," "We're Coming in Loaded."

Running time: 106 minutes
Release date: 11/2/62

Laurel Goodwin, Elvis Presley

It Happened at the World's Fair

Metro-Goldwyn-Mayer

Credits

Directed by Norman Taurog.
Written by Si Rose and Seaman Jacobs.
Photographed by Joseph Ruttenberg, A.S.C.
Edited by Fredric Steinkamp.
Music Score by Leith Stevens.
Art Direction by George W. Davis and Preston Ames.
Musical Numbers Staged by Jack Baker.
Makeup by William Tuttle.
Vocal Backgrounds by The Jordanaires and The Mello Men.
Asistant Director: Al Jennings.
Technical Advisor: Colonel Tom Parker.
A Ted Richmond Production.
Photographed in Panavision and Metrocolor.

Cast

Mike Edwards	Elvis Presley
Diane Warren	Joan O'Brien
Danny Burke	Gary Lockwood
Sue-Lin	Vicky Tiu
Vince Bradley	H. M. Wynant
Miss Steuben	Edith Atwater
Barney Thatcher	Guy Raymond
Miss Ettinger	Dorothy Green
Walter Ling	Kam Tong
Dorothy Johnson	Yvonne Craig

Synopsis

Elvis, a bush pilot, and his sidekick Gary Lockwood, hitchhike to Seattle to find a job in order to reclaim their plane, which a sheriff has attached as security.

Joan O'Brien, Elvis Presley

Yvonne Craig, Elvis Presley

Joan O'Brien, Elvis Presley

Joan O'Brien, Elvis Presley

Elvis finds himself involved with two "dates": the first with Vicky Tiu, little daughter of a Chinese farmer whom he takes on a tour of the Seattle World's Fair; the second with Joan O'Brien, attractive nurse at the dispensary.

A series of complications takes place when Elvis unexpectedly finds himself in the role of Vicky's guardian and later comes to believe that Joan O'Brien has given him a double-cross. But all comes out happily in the climax in which the two pilots narrowly escape being made the victims of a smuggling deal.

Songs
"I'm Falling in Love Tonight," "Relax," "How Would You Like to Be," "Beyond the Bend," "One Broken Heart for Sale," "Cotton Candy Land," "A World of Our Own," "Take Me to the Fair," "They Remind Me Too Much of You," "Happy Ending."

Running time: 105 minutes
Release date: 4/3/63

Gary Lockwood, Elvis Presley

Vicky Tiu, Elvis Presley

Joan O'Brien, Elvis Presley

Fun In Acapulco
Paramount

Credits
Produced by Hal B. Wallis.
Directed by Richard Thorpe.
Screenplay by Allan Weiss.
Photographed by Daniel L. Fapp, A.S.C.
Edited by Warren Low, A.C.E.
Costumes by Edith Head.
Art Direction by Hal Pereira and Walter Tyler.
Technical Advisor: Colonel Tom Parker.
Color by Technicolor.

Cast
Mike Windgren	Elvis Presley
Margarita Dauphine	Ursula Andress
Dolores Gomez	Elsa Cardenas
Maximillian	Paul Lukas
Raoul Almeido	Larry Domasin
Moreno	Alejandro Rey
Jose	Robert Carricart
Jamie Harkins	Teri Hope

Synopsis
Elvis arrives in Acapulco as a sailor on a motor yacht. He is escaping from a tragic incident in the States where, as a trapeze artist, he caused his partner to be seriously injured.

In Acapulco, a young shoe-shine boy, Larry Domasin, hears Elvis sing and volunteers to become his manager. He succeeds in getting Elvis hired as a singer in a swank resort hotel.

Elvis soon becomes romantically involved with two beautiful women: Elsa Cardenas, a lady bullfighter;

Ursula Andress, Elvis Presley, Elsa Cardenas

Ursula Andress, Larry Domasin, Elvis Presley

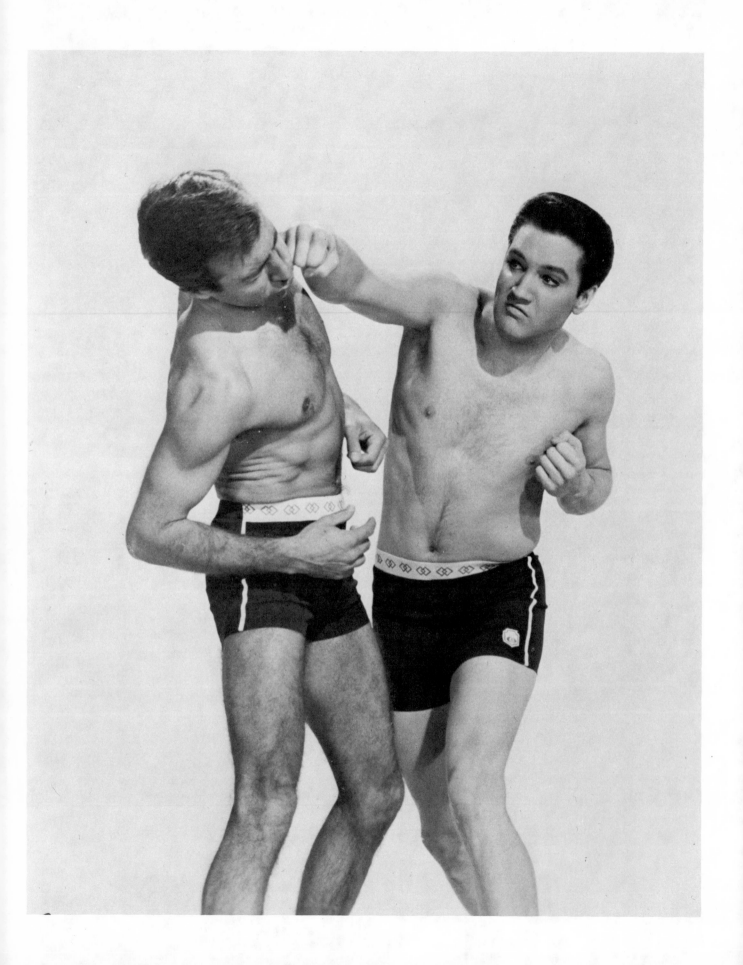

and Ursula Andress, the hotel's social director. In addition to singing every night, Elvis has to work as a lifeguard at the hotel swimming pool. The regular lifeguard, Alejandro Rey, likes Ursula and resents having Elvis around. One day, Elvis tries to dive from the high board, but cannot, because he remembers the fateful day when he dropped his circus partner. Alejandro notices Elvis's fear of heights, and after some sleuthing finds out the true story.

Every night Alejandro does a spectacular plunge off the cliffs, 136 feet into the raging surf. One evening, Alejandro and Elvis have an argument which develops into a fight. Elvis wins, but Alejandro pretends to be hurt.

Elvis decides to overcome his fear of heights and makes the dive himself. As the onlookers applaud him wildly, Elvis rushes out of the water to embrace Ursula and proposes they go to Florida.

Songs

"Fun in Acapulco," "Vino, Dinero y Amor," "Mexico," "El Toro," "Marguerita," "The Bullfighter Was a Lady," "No Room to Rhumba in a Sports Car," "I Think I'm Gonna Like It Here," "Bossa Nova Baby," "You Can't Say No in Acapulco," "Guadalajara."

Running time: 98 minutes
Release date: 11/21/63

On the set of "Fun in Acapulco"

Elvis Presley and Ursula Andress

146

Kissin' Cousins

Metro-Goldwyn-Mayer

Credits

Produced by Sam Katzman.
Directed by Gene Nelson.
Screenplay by Gerald Drayson
Adams and Gene Nelson.
Story by Gerald Drayson Adams.
Photographed by Ellis W. Carter,
A.S.C.
Edited by Ben Lewis.
Music Supervised and Conducted by
Fred Karger.
Choreography by Hal Belfer.
Art Direction by George W. Davis
and Eddie Imazu.
Makeup by William Tuttle.
Assistant Director: Eli Dunn.
Technical Advisor: Colonel Tom
Parker.
A Four Leaf Production.
Photographed in Panavision and
Metrocolor.

Elvis Presley and Elvis Presley

Yvonne Craig, Elvis Presley

Elvis Presley, Glenda Farrell, Pam Austin, Arthur O'Connell
and Yvonne Craig

Elvis Presley, Yvonne Craig, Donald Woods

Top Row: Pam Austin, Glenda Farrell, Yvonne Craig
Bottom Row: Elvis Presley, Arthur O'Connell, Hound Dog, Elvis Presley

Cynthia Pepper, Elvis Presley

Cast

Josh Morgan
Jodie Tatum } ...... Elvis Presley
Pappy Tatum ... Arthur O'Connell
Ma Tatum .... Glenda Farrell
Capt. Robert Salbo..Jack Alvertson
Selena Tatum .... Pam Austin
Midge .... Cynthia Pepper
Azalea Tatum ...... Yvonne Craig
General Donford .. Donald Woods
Sgt. Bailey .... Tommy Farrell
Trudy .... Beverly Powers
Dixie .... Hortense Petra
General's Aide ..... Robert Stone

Synopsis

Elvis is an Air Force officer who tries to persuade a highly independent hillbilly family to sell their land to the government for use as a missile site. The Tatum family—Arthur O'Connell, Glenda Farrell, Pam Austin, Yvonne Craig, and Elvis (as the blond Jodie)—don't want any part of the government snooping around their mountain and interfering with their moonshine-making activities.

Elvis (as the officer) romances Yvonne Craig, and Elvis (as the hillbilly) romances Cynthia Pepper, a WAC. After a half-dozen songs and several dance numbers, everything turns out for the best: the government gets the mountain and Elvis gets the girl.

Songs

"Kissin' Cousins," "One Boy, Two Little Girls," "There's Gold in the Mountains," "Catchin' On Fast," "Barefoot Ballad," "Once Is Enough," "Smoky Mountain Boy," "Tender Feeling."

Running time: 96 minutes
Release date: 3/6/64

Viva
Las
Vegas

Metro-Goldwyn-Mayer

Elvis Presley, Ann-Margret

Credits

Produced by Jack Cummings and
George Sidney.
Directed by George Sidney.
Screenplay by Sally Benton.
Photographed by Joseph Biroc,
A.S.C.
Edited by John McSweeney, Jr.
Music by George Stoll.
Costumes by Don Feld.
Choreography by David Winters.
Makeup by William Tuttle.
Assistant Director: Milton Feldman.
Technical Advisor: Colonel Tom
Parker.
A Jack Cummings–George Sidney
Production.
Photographed in Panavision and
Metrocolor.

Ann-Margret, Elvis Presley

Ann-Margret, Elvis Presley

Ann-Margret, Elvis Presley

Cast

Lucky Jordan . . . . . . Elvis Presley
Rusty Martin . . . . Ann-Margret
Count Elmo Mancini

Cesare Danova
Mr. Martin . . . . . William Demarest
Shorty Farnsworth . . . . Nicky Blair

Synopsis

Elvis arrives in Las Vegas for the big Grand Prix race, but has engine trouble. He also falls in love at first sight, with a girl, Ann-Margret. Not knowing her name or address and assuming she is one of the showgirls in Las Vegas, Elvis and his racing rival, Cesare Danova, search various nightclubs for the girl. Unable to find her, they return to the hotel and Elvis spots the girl again. She is the swimming instructor at the hotel pool. He starts singing and romanc-ing her, while repairing his engine and finally winning the Big Race.

Songs

"Viva Las Vegas," "If You Think I Don't Need You," "The Lady Loves Me," "I Need Somebody to Lean On," "C'mon Everybody," "Tomorrow and Forever," "Santa Lucia."

Running time: 86 minutes
Release date: 4/20/64

"This fetching entertainment may not rate that exclamation point, but it is one of several Elvis Presley musical frolics that can hold its head high enough, with no apologies."

—Howard Thompson,
The New York Times
Guide to Movies on TV

Ann-Margret, Elvis Presley

Roustabout

Paramount

Barbara Stanwyck, Elvis Presley

158

Barbara Stanwyck, Elvis Presley, Joan Freeman

Elvis Presley, Barbara Stanwyck, Joan Freeman, Leif Erickson

Credits

Produced by Hal B. Wallis.
Associate Producer: Paul Nathan.
Directed by John Rich.
Screenplay by Anthony Lawrence
and Allan Weiss.
Story by Allan Weiss.
Photographed by Lucien Ballard,
A.S.C.
Music by Joseph L. Lilley.
Costumes by Edith Head.
Art Direction by Hal Pereira and
Walter Tyler.
Musical Numbers Staged by Earl
Barton.
Assistant Director: D. Michael
Moore.
Technical Advisor: Colonel Tom
Parker.
Photographed in Techniscope and
Technicolor.

Cast

Charlie Rogers . . . . . . Elvis Presley
Maggie Morgan . Barbara Stanwyck
Cathy Lean . . . . Joan Freeman
Joe Lean . . . . Leif Erickson
Madame Mijanou
                    Sue Ane Langdon
Harry Carver . . . . Pat Buttram
Marge . . . . Joan Staley
Arthur Nielson . . . . Dabs Greer
Fred . . . . Steve Brodie
Sam . . . . Norman Grabowski
Lou . . . . Jack Albertson
Hazel . . . . Jane Dulo
Cody Marsh . . . . Joel Fluellen
Little Egypt . . . . Wilda Taylor

Synopsis

Elvis, a singer at an espresso café,
gets into a fight with three unruly
characters and after expertly dis-

Elvis Presley, Joan Freeman

patching them with karate, leaves the nightspot and heads for points unknown on his motorcycle. After wandering a bit, Elvis gets a job as a "roustabout" or handyman in a carnival run by Barbara Stanwyck. At the carnival Elvis meets Joan Freeman and falls for her.

Business at the carnival is practically nil, so, in between jobs, Elvis breaks into an impromptu song on the midway. News of this gets around and suddenly droves of young people flock to the carnival. A new career is launched for Elvis.

Things soon sour when Elvis gets into a fight with one of the customers and decides to leave the carnival. He feels all washed up and sure that he has lost Joan Freeman, so he heads

for a rival carnival which had previously made him an offer.

With Elvis gone, Barbara Stanwyck's carnival takes a nose dive and the creditors come knocking at its doors. With only one chance left, Joan goes to Elvis and persuades him to return and save the carnival.

Songs

"Roustabout," "Poison Ivy League," "Wheels on My Heels," "It's a Wonderful World," "It's Carnival Time," "Carny Town," "One Track Heart," "Hard Knocks," "Little Egypt," "Big Love, Big Heartache," "There's a Brand New Day on the Horizon."

Running time: 101 minutes
Release date: 11/12/64

Girl Happy
Metro-Goldwyn-Mayer

Credits
Produced by Joe Pasternak.
Directed by Boris Sagal.
Written by Harvey Bullock and
  R. S. Allen.
Photographed by Philip H. Lathrop,
  A.S.C.
Edited by Rita Roland.
Music by George Stoll.
Art Direction by George D. Davis
  and Addison Hehr.
Makeup by William Tuttle.
Assistant Director: Jack Aldworth
Technical Advisor: Colonel Tom
  Parker.
A Joe Pasternak Production.
A Euterpe Picture.
Photographed in Panavision and
  Metrocolor.

Cast
Rusty Wells . . . . Elvis Presley
Valerie . . . . Shelley Fabares
Big Frank . . . . Harold J. Stone
Andy . . . . Gary Crosby
Wilbur . . . . Jody Baker
Sunny Daze . . . . Nita Talbot
Deena . . . . Mary Ann Mobley
Romano . . . . Fabrizio Mioni
Doc . . . . Jimmy Hawkins
Sgt. Benson . . . . Jackie Coogan
Brentwood Von Durgenfeld
                    Peter Brooks
Mr. Penchill . . . . John Fiedler
Betsy . . . . Chris Noel
Laurie . . . . Lyn Edington
Nancy . . . . Gale Gilmore
Bobbie . . . . Pamela Curran
Linda . . . . Rusty Allen

Synopsis
Elvis is hired by Chicago nightclub owner Harold Stone to keep an eye on his daughter, Shelley Fabares, while she is on vacation in Fort Lauderdale. The job involves Elvis in one complication after another.

Gary Crosby, Elvis Presley, Jody Baker

Elvis Presley, Mary Ann Mobley

Elvis Presley, Mary Ann Mobley

Harold J. Stone, Elvis Presley

There is a riot in a nightclub; Elvis interrupts a shipboard rendezvous between Shelley and her amorous admirer Fabrizio Mioni by removing the cruiser from the water, trundling it through the streets of the resort town, and depositing Shelley in her room. After Shelley gets arrested for disorderly conduct at a nightclub, Elvis digs a tunnel under the jail to get her out. Finally Elvis succumbs to Shelley's charms and all ends well.

Songs

"Girl Happy," "Spring Fever," "Fort Lauderdale Chamber of Commerce," "Startin' Tonight," "Wolf Call," "Do Not Disturb," "Cross My Heart and Hope to Die," "She's the Meanest Girl in Town," "Do the Clam," "Puppet on a String," "I've Got to Find My Baby."

Running time: 96 minutes
Release date: 1/22/65

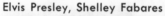

Elvis Presley, Shelley Fabares

Tickle Me

Allied Artists

Credits

Produced by Ben Schwalb.
Directed by Norman Taurog.
Story and Screenplay by Elwood
 Ullman and Edward Bernds.
Photographed by Loyal Griggs.
Edited by Archie Marshek.
Music Director: Walter Scharf.

Art Direction by Arthur Lonergan.
Choreography by David Winters.
Makeup by Frank Westmore and
 Bill Reynolds.
Assistant Director: Artie Jacobson.
Technical Advisor: Colonel Tom
 Parker.
Photographed in Panavision and
 DeLuxe Color.

ALLIED ARTISTS PICTURE CORPORATION PRESENTS

ELVIS PRESLEY
in
"TICKLE ME" (U)
Co-starring
JULIE ADAMS   JOCELYN LANE   JACK MULLANEY
PANAVISION®   DE LUXE COLOR®
RELEASED BY WARNER-PATHE DISTRIBUTORS LTD.

Elvis Presley, Jocelyn Lane

Elvis Presley and a bevy of beauties

Cast

Lonnie Beale . . . . Elvis Presley
Pam Merritt . . . . Jocelyn Lane
Vera Radford . . . . Julie Adams
Stanley Potter . . . . . Jack Mullaney
Estelle Penfield . . . . Merry Anders
Hilda . . . . Connie Gilchrist
Brad Bentley . . . . Edward Faulkner
Deputy Sturdivant . . . Bill Williams
Henry . . . . Louis Elias
Adolph . . . . John Dennis
Janet . . . . Laurie Burton
Clair Kinnamon . . . . Linda Rogers
Sibyl . . . . Ann Morell
Ronnie . . . . Lilyan Chauvin
Evelyn . . . . Jean Ingram
Mildred . . . . Francine York
Pat . . . . Eve Bruce

Synopsis

Elvis is a singing rodeo rider who drifts into an expensive dude ranch and beauty spa patronized by wealthy glamour girls. The owner, Julie Adams, hires Elvis as a handyman. Jocelyn Lane has a letter from her late grandfather directing her to a cache of gold in the ghost town of Silverado. The sheriff, Bill Williams, and his gang learn of the letter and plot to take it away from Jocelyn. Elvis comes to her rescue, battling the gang in a free-for-all in the ghost town. After subduing the crooks, Elvis and Jocelyn find the gold and decide to get married.

Songs

"Night Rider," "I'm Yours," "I Feel I've Known You Forever," "Dirty, Dirty Feeling," "Put the Blame on Me," "Easy Question," "Slowly But Surely."

Running time: 90 minutes
Release date: 6/15/65

Harum Scarum
Metro-Goldwyn-Mayer

Credits
Produced by Sam Katzman.
Directed by Gene Nelson.
Written by Gerald Drayson Adams.
Photographed by Fred H. Jackman.
Edited by Ben Levin.
Music Supervised and Conducted by
   Fred Karger.
Choreography by Earl Barton.
Art Direction by George W. Davis
   and H. McClure Capps.
Makeup by William Tuttle.
Technical Advisor: Colonel Tom
   Parker.
A Four Leaf Production.
Color by Metrocolor.

Fran Jeffries, Elvis Presley

Cast

Johnny Tyronne	Elvis Presley
Princess Shalimar	Mary Ann Mobley
Aishah	Fran Jeffries
Prince Drana	Michael Ansara
Zacha	Jay Novello
King Toranshad	Philip Reed
Sinan	Theo Marcuse
Baba	Billy Barty
Mohar	Dirk Harvey
Juina	Jack Castanzo
Captain Heret	Larry Chance
Leilah	Barbara Werle
Emerald	Brenda Benet
Sapphire	Gail Gilmore
Amethyst	Wilda Taylor
Sari	Vicki Malkin

Synopsis

Elvis is a motion picture and recording star, who is kidnapped by a band of assassins while on a personal appearance tour of the Middle East. Suddenly he finds himself involved in a plot to murder the king, becomes the rescuing hero of maidens in distress, flings himself into adventure with a gang of pickpockets and rogues. Elvis also finds time to ward off the advances of the predatory Aishah and falls in love with the Princess Shalimar.

It all turns out merrily and melodically well, with Elvis saving the king from assassination, winning the beautiful princess and, at the finish, returns to the U.S.A. with an Oriental dancing troupe which becomes a part of his Las Vegas act.

Songs

"Harem Holiday," "My Desert Serenade," "Go East—Young Man," "Mirage," "Kismet," "Shake the Tambourine," "Hey Little Girl," "Golden Coins," "So Close, Yet So Far (from Paradise)."

Running time: 95 minutes
Release date: 12/15/65

Frankie and Johnny

United Artists

Credits

Produced by Edward Small.
Directed by Fred de Cordova.
Screenplay by Alex Gottlieb.
Story by Nat Perrin.
Photographed by Jacques Marquette, A.S.C.
Edited by Grant Whytock.
Art Direction by Walter Simonds.
Dance Director: Earl Barton.
Musical Director: Fred Karger.
Makeup by Dan Greenway.
Technical Advisor: Colonel Tom Parker.
An Edward Small Production.
Color by Technicolor.

Cast

Johnny .... Elvis Presley
Frankie .... Donna Douglas
Nellie Bly .... Nancy Kovack
Mitzi .... Sue Ane Langdon
Braden .... Anthony Eisley
Cully .... Harry Morgan
Pog .... Audrey Christie
Blackie .... Robert Strauss
Wilbur .... Jerome Cowan
Earl Barton Dancers
    Wilda Taylor, Larri Thomas, Dee Jay Mattis, Judy Chapman

Synopsis

Donna Douglas loves Elvis but he loves gambling almost as much as he does Donna. She refuses to marry him until he stops betting and losing every cent he makes. Together they earn a living singing on the Mississippi gambling-showboat owned by Anthony Eisley.

Elvis Presley, Donna Douglas, Nancy Kovack

Harry Morgan, Elvis Presley, Donna Douglas, Nancy Kovack

Harry Morgan, Elvis Presley, Nancy Kovack

Donna Douglas, Elvis Presley

When a gypsy fortune-teller tells Elvis that he can change his losing streak with a new redhead who's coming into his life, Elvis becomes interested. The redhead turns out to be Eisley's old flame, Nancy Kovack. Donna becomes jealous of Nancy and Eisley becomes jealous of Elvis, especially when Nancy uses Elvis to try to get Eisley to marry her.

Elvis's piano-playing sidekick, Harry Morgan, writes a new song, "Frankie and Johnny," that is introduced on the showboat, and it looks like Elvis and Donna will make it big and finally go to Broadway.

Just as the fortune-teller predicted, Elvis wins a fortune with Nancy beside him, but Donna angrily throws all the money away. Then Eisley's henchman, trying to help his boss, puts a real bullet in the gun that Donna uses to "kill" Elvis in the finish of the title song.

But a lucky charm that Elvis wears saves his life, and Donna decides that she loves Elvis no matter how much he gambles.

Songs
"Frankie and Johnny," "Come Along," "Petunia, the Gardener's Daughter," "Chesay," "What Every Woman Lives For," "Look Out, Broadway," "Beginner's Luck," "Down by the Riverside," "When The Saints Go Marching In," "Shout It Out," "Hard Luck," "Please Don't Stop Loving Me," "Everybody Come Aboard."

Running time: 87 minutes
Release date: 7/20/66

Paradise – Hawaiian Style

Paramount

Elvis Presley, Linda Wong

Credits

Produced by Hal Wallis.
Associate Producer: Paul Nathan.
Directed by Michael Moore.
Screenplay by Allan Weiss and
 Anthony Lawrence.
From an Original Story by Allan
 Weiss.
Photographed by W. Wallace Kelley,
 A.S.C.
Edited by Warren Low, A.C.E.
Background Music by Joseph J.
 Lilley.
Choreography by Jack Regas.
Costumes by Edith Head.
Art Direction by Hal Pereira and
 Walter Tyler.
Technical Advisor: Colonel Tom
 Parker.
Color by Technicolor.

Cast

Rick Richards . . . . Elvis Presley
Judy Hudson . . . . . . Suzanne Leigh
Danny Kohana . . . . . James Shigeta
Jan Kohana . . . Donna Butterworth
Lani . . . . Marianna Hill
Pua . . . . Irene Tsu
Lehua . . . . Linda Wong
Joanna . . . . Julie Parrish
Betty Kohana . . . . Jan Shepard
Donald Belden . . . . . John Doucette
Moki . . . . Philip Ahn
Mr. Cubberson . . . . . Grady Sutton
Andy Lowell . . . . Don Collier
Mrs. Barrington . . . . . Doris Packer
Mrs. Belden . . . . Mary Treen
Peggy Holdren . . . . . Gigi Verone

Suzanne Leigh, Elvis Presley

Suzanne Leigh, Marianna Hill, Elvis Presley

Elvis Presley, Irene Tsu

Synopsis

Elvis and his buddy James Shigeta start a helicopter charter service in Hawaii. Elvis has three gorgeous girls—Linda Wong, Marianna Hill, Julie Parrish—steering customers to his charter service, and business is so good Elvis hires Suzanne Leigh as a secretary.

While taking a girlfriend for a ride in his helicopter, Elvis loses control and doesn't regain it till the careening chopper has forced an automobile into a ditch. The driver of the car is John Doucette of the Federal Aviation Agency and Elvis is grounded till further notice.

Elvis finds that James Shigeta and his daughter Donna Butterworth had a crash landing, and Elvis flies to the rescue. The newspapers have reported the rescue, and the aviation board may cancel Elvis's flying license permanently.

Elvis goes to see John Doucette and explains everything, and the FAA agent assures him that because of the mitigating circumstances of the rescue he will not lose his license.

Songs

"Paradise, Hawaiian Style," "House of Sand," "Queenie Wahine's Papaya," "You Scratch My Back," "Drums of the Islands," "It's a Dog's Life," "Datin'," "Stop Where You Are," "This Is My Heaven."

Running time: 91 minutes
Release date: 6/8/66

Spinout
Metro-Goldwyn-Mayer

Carl Betz, Elvis Presley, Shelley Fabares

Credits

Produced by Joe Pasternak.
Directed by Norman Taurog.
Written by Theodore J. Flicker and George Kirgo.
Photographed by Daniel L. Fapp, A.S.C.
Edited by Rita Roland.
Music by George Stoll.
Musical Numbers Staged by Jack Baker.
Vocal backgrounds by The Jordanaires.
Art Direction by George W. Davis and Edward Carfagno.
Makeup by William Tuttle.
Associate Producer: Hank Moonjean.
Technical Advisor: Colonel Tom Parker.
A Joe Pasternak Production.
A Euterpe Picture.
Photographed in Panavision and Metrocolor.

Cast

Mike McCoy . . . . Elvis Presley
Cynthia Foxhugh . . Shelley Fabares
Diane St. Clair . . . . . Diane McBain
Les . . . . Deborah Walley
Susan . . . . Dodie Marshall
Curly . . . . Jack Mullaney
Lt. Tracy Richards . . Will Hutchins
Philip Short . . . . . Warren Berlinger
Larry . . . . Jimmy Hawkins
Howard Foxhugh . . . . . . Carl Betz
Bernard Ranley . . . . Cecil Kellaway
Violet Ranley . . . . Una Merkel
Blodgett . . . . Frederic Warlock
Harry . . . . Dave Barry

Jimmy Hawkins, Jack Mullaney, Deborah Walley, Elvis Presley

Diane McBain, Elvis Presley, Deborah Walley, Shelley Fabares

Elvis Presley, Shelley Fabares

Deborah Walley, Elvis Presley, Jimmy Hawkins

Elvis Presley, Una Merkel, Cecil Kellaway

Synopsis

Four girls chase after Elvis. Shelley Fabares is the pert, spoiled daughter of a millionaire, who always gets what she wants, and she wants Elvis, leader of a touring combo. Diane McBain is a best-selling author, researching her next book, *The Perfect American Male,* and when she meets Elvis, she decides she has found her subject. Deborah Walley is the cute drummer in Elvis's band, whose heart is drumming for her boss, while Dodie Marshall ends up as the latest beauty to try to corral Elvis into matrimony.

When not being chased by girls, Elvis sings and races over mountain roads. After a few humorous situations, Elvis manages to eat his cake and have it, so to speak. He marries all four girls.

Songs

"Spinout," "I'll Be Back," "All That I Am," "Am I Ready," "Stop, Look, Listen."

Running time: 95 minutes
Release date: 12/14/66

Elvis and bathing beauties

Easy Come, Easy Go

Paramount

Dodie Marshall, Elvis Presley

Credits

Produced by Hal Wallis.
Associate Producer: Paul Nathan.
Directed by John Rich.
Screenplay by Allan Weiss and
    Anthony Lawrence.
Photographed by William Margulies,
    A.S.C.
Edited by Archie Marshek, A.C.E.
Background Score by Joseph J.
    Lilley.
Vocal Accompaniment by The
    Jordanaires.
Choreography by David Winters.
Costumes by Edith Head.
Art Direction by Hal Pereira and
    Walter Tyler.
Sound by John Carter and
    Charles Grenzback.
Technical Advisor: Colonel Tom
    Parker.
Color by Technicolor.

Cast

Ted Jackson . . . . Elvis Presley
Jo Symington . . . . . Dodie Marshall
Dina Bishop . . . . Pat Priest
Judd Whitman . . . . Pat Harrington
Gil Carey . . . . Skip Ward
Schwartz . . . . Sandy Kenyon
Captain Jack . . . . . Frank McHugh
Cooper . . . . Ed Griffith
Ship's Officers
        Reed Morgan, Mickey Elley
Vicki . . . . Elaine Beckett
Mary . . . . Shari Nims
Zoltan . . . . Diki Lawrence
Artist . . . . Robert Lawrence
Madame Neherina . Elsa Lanchester

Elvis Presley, Dodie Marshall

Elvis Presley, Elsa Lanchester

Elvis Presley, Dodie Marshall

Synopsis

Navy frogman Elvis Presley discovers a treasure chest in the hull of an old ship. He calls on Frank McHugh, an expert on nautical lore, to find some information on the cargo of the sunken ship. Frank tells Elvis that Dodie Marshall, the only descendant of the ship's skipper, would know that.

Dodie, a yoga student and go-go dancer at the local discotheque, confirms the fact that the cargo was coffee and a valuable chest of Spanish pieces-of-eight. She agrees to help Elvis if the money is given to the town's art center.

Discharged from the Navy, Elvis tries to reclaim the chest. He goes into partnership with Pat Harrington, and sings at his club as part of the deal. Meanwhile playgirl Pat Priest and her boyfriend Skip Ward have their eyes on the treasure and kidnap Elvis's equipment and Frank McHugh. Elvis pursues the pirates, has a fight or two and recovers the treasure chest. When the chest is opened, the coins are copper rather than gold, and worth less than $4,000. The money goes as a down payment for an art center, and Elvis wins the girl.

Songs

"Easy Come, Easy Go," "The Love Machine," "Yoga Is As Yoga Does," "You Gotta Stop," "Sing, You Children," "I'll Take Love."

Running time: 95 minutes
Release date: 6/14/67

Double Trouble

Metro-Goldwyn-Mayer

Credits

Produced by Judd Bernard and
 Irwin Winkler.
Directed by Norman Taurog.
Screenplay by Jo Heims.
Based on a Story by Marc Brandel.
Photographed by Daniel L. Fapp,
 A.S.C.
Edited by John McSweeney.
Music Score by Jeff Alexander.
Art Direction by George W. Davis
 and Merrill Pye.
Choreography by Alex Romero.
Special Visual Effects by
 J. McMillian Johnson and
 Carroll L. Shepphird.
Makeup by William Tuttle.
Assistant Director: Claude Binyon, Jr.
Technical Advisor: Colonel Tom
 Parker.
A B.C.W. Picture.
Photographed in Panavision and
 Metrocolor.

Cast

Guy Lambert . . . . Elvis Presley
Jill Conway . . . . Annette Day
Gerald Waverly . . . . John Williams
Claire Dunham . . Yvonne Romain
The Wiere Brothers . . . Themselves
Archie Brown . . . . . Chips Rafferty
Arthur Babcock . Norman Rossington
Georgie . . . . Monty Landis
Morley . . . . Michael Murphy
Inspector DeGrotte . . . Leon Askin
Iceman . . . . John Alderson
Captain Roach . . . . Stanley Adams
The G Men . . . . Themselves

Elvis Presley, Annette Day

Yvonne Romain, Elvis Presley

Elvis Presley, Annette Day

Annette Day, Elvis Presley

The Wiere Brothers, Elvis Presley

Synopsis

Elvis heads a musical act at a London night club, where one of his fans, Annette Day, falls in love with him. John Williams, her guardian, is determined to break up the romance and packs her off to a school in Brussels, Belgium, not realizing that Elvis has a singing engagement there. And from the moment they meet again on the boat crossing the English Channel, the lovers find themselves engulfed in an unremitting series of adventures and predicaments as they are followed by a trio of detectives, the Wiere Brothers, each suspecting Elvis of jewel smuggling.

Songs

"Double Trouble," "Baby, If You Give Me All Your Love," "Could I Fall in Love," "Long-Legged Girls with Short Dresses On," "City of Night," "Old MacDonald," "I Love Only One Girl," "There's So Much World to See," "It Won't Be Long."

Running time: 90 minutes
Release date: 5/24/67

Clambake

United Artists

Credits

Produced by Levy-Gardner-Laven
    Productions.
Directed by Arthur Nadel.
Story and Screenplay by Arthur
    Brown, Jr.
Photographed by William Margulies,
    A.S.C.
Edited by Tom Rolf.
Music by Jeff Alexander.
Technical Advisor: Colonel Tom
    Parker.
Photographed in Techniscope and
    Technicolor.

Cast

Scott Heywood ...... Elvis Presley
Dianne Carter .... Shelley Fabares
Tom Wilson .... Will Hutchins
James Jamison III ...... Bill Bixby
Sam Burton .... Gary Merrill
Duster Heywood ... James Gregory
Ellie .... Amanda Harley
Sally .... Suzy Kaye
Gloria .... Angelique Pettyjohn

Bill Bixby, Shelley Fabares, Will Hutchins

EP-6 (12-4R)

Will Hutchins, Elvis Presley

Synopsis

Elvis Presley, millionaire's son, leaves home to see if he can accomplish something worthwhile on his own. En route to Miami Beach, he exchanges identities with Will Hutchins, a poor water-ski instructor.

Elvis's first student is Shelley Fabares, who is in Miami to catch a rich husband and sets her sights on Bill Bixby, a playboy and boat racer. Elvis becomes jealous when Bixby becomes interested in Shelley and becomes determined to impress the girl.

Unable to fall back on his wealth, Elvis forms a partnership with Gary Merrill, who owns a new design craft that mysteriously ripped apart in the previous year's boat race. Elvis perfects a hardener for the protective coating on the ship and the craft is ready to race. Unable to test it before the race, Elvis risks life and limb in the effort to win the race and the girl.

Songs

"Clambake," "Who Needs Money," "A House That Has Everything," "Confidence," "Hey, Hey, Hey," "You Don't Know Me," "The Girl I Never Loved."

Running Time: 99 minutes
Release date: 12/4/67

Stay Away, Joe

Metro-Goldwyn-Mayer

Elvis Presley, Quentin Dean

188

Credits

Produced by Douglas Laurence.
Directed by Peter Tewksbury.
Screenplay by Michael A. Hoey.
Based on the Novel by Dan
Cushman.
Photographed by Fred Koenekamp,
A.S.C.
Edited by George W. Brooks.
Music Score by Jack Marshall.
Art Direction by George W. Davis
and Carl Anderson.
Vocal backgrounds by The
Jordanaires.
Makeup by William Tuttle.
Assistant Director: Dale Hutchinson.
Technical Advisor: Colonel Tom
Parker.
Photographed in Panavision and
Metrocolor.

Cast

Joe Lightcloud . . . . . . Elvis Presley
Charlie Lightcloud . Burgess Meredith
Glenda Callahan . . . . Joan Blondell
Annie Lightcloud . . . . Katy Jurado
Grandpa . . . . Thomas Gomez
Hy Slager . . . . Henry Jones
Bronc Hoverty . . . . L. Q. Jones
Mamie Callahan . . . . Quentin Dean
Mrs. Hawkins . . . . . Anne Seymour
Congressman Morissey
                Douglas Henderson
Lorne Hawkins . . . . Angus Duncan
Frank Hawk . . . . Michael Lane
Mary Lightcloud . . Susan Trustman
Hike Bowers . . . . . Warren Vanders
Bull Shortgun . . . . . Buck Kartalian
Connie Shortgun . . . . . . Mourishka
Marlene Standing Rattle . Caitlin Wyles
Billie-Joe Hump . . . Marya Christen
Jackson He-Crow . Del "Sonny" West
Little Deer . . . . Jennifer Peak
Deputy Sheriff Matson . Brett Parker
Orville Witt . . . . Michael Keller

Elvis Presley, Quentin Dean

Burgess Meredith, Katy Jurado, Susan Trustman,
Elvis Presley and Thomas Gomez

L. Q. Jones, Elvis Presley

Katy Jurado, Elvis Presley

Synopsis

Elvis, a Navajo Indian, returns from the rodeo circuit to his Arizona reservation with twenty heifers and a bull he promoted from his Congressman. The idea was that if Elvis and his Indian father, Burgess Meredith, were successful in raising cattle, the U.S. government would help the whole reservation. Elvis barbecues the bull and sells the cows to buy some plumbing and other home improvements his stepmother, Katy Jurado, wants.

Joan Blondell is a gun-totin' tavern owner who chases Elvis all over the county in the effort to keep him from her not-too-bright daughter, Quentin Dean. When not chasing that girl, Elvis chases the girlfriends of his fellow braves. Finally, after a series of comic vicissitudes, when it appears that the family will go to jail for selling government property (the cattle), Elvis saves the day.

Songs

"Stay Away, Joe," "Dominique."

Running time: 98 minutes
Release date: 3/14/68

Quentin Dean, Joan Blondell, Elvis Presley

Quentin Dean, Elvis Presley

Elvis Presley, Katy Jurado, Burgess Meredith

Speedway
Metro-Goldwyn-Mayer

Nancy Sinatra, Elvis Presley

Nancy Sinatra, Elvis Presley

Credits

Produced by Douglas Laurence.
Directed by Norman Taurog.
Written by Phillip Shuken.
Photographed by Joseph Ruttenberg,
 A.S.C.
Edited by Russell Farrell.
Music Score by Jeff Alexander.
Art Direction by George W. Davis
 and Leroy Coleman.
Makeup by William Tuttle.
Special Visual Effects by Carroll L.
 Shepphird.
Vocal Background by The
 Jordanaires.
Assistant Director: Dale Hutchinson.
Technical Advisor: Colonel Tom
 Parker.
Photographed in Panavision and
 Metrocolor.

Bill Bixby, Elvis Presley, Nancy Sinatra,
Carl Ballantine, Ponice Ponce

Cast

Steve Grayson . . . . Elvis Presley
Susan Jacks . . . . Nancy Sinatra
Kenny Donford . . . . Bill Bixby
R. W. Hepworth . . . . Gale Gordon
Abel Esterlake . William Schallert
Ellie Esterlake . . Victoria Meyerink
Paul Dado . . . . Ross Hagen
Birdie Kebner . . . . . Carl Ballantine
Juan Medala . . . . Ponice Ponce
The Cook . . . . Harry Hickox
Billie Jo . . . . Christopher West
Mary Ann . . . . . Miss Beverly Hills
Ted Simmons . . . . . . Harper Carter
Lloyd Meadows . . . . Bob Harris
Carrie . . . . Courtney Brown
Billie . . . . Dana Brown
Annie . . . . Patti Jean Keith
Mike . . . . Carl Reindel
Dumb Blonde . . . . Gari Hardy
Lori . . . . Charlotte Considine
Race Announcer . . . . . Sandy Reed

Nancy Sinatra, Elvis Presley

196

Nancy Sinatra, Elvis Presley

Synopsis

Elvis is a stock car racing champion whose prowess on the track is matched by his generosity in sharing his winnings with people in need. Partly as the result of his philanthropies but more largely due to the fact that his manager, Bill Bixby, has been losing Elvis's winnings by betting on slow horses, Elvis finds himself·spectacularly in arrears on his income tax payments. The Internal Revenue Service sends Nancy Sinatra to check up on Elvis and straighten everything out.

After a few misunderstandings, all the plot twists are unraveled; Elvis begins paying back his income tax and wins Nancy.

Songs

"Speedway," "Let Yourself Go," "Your Time Hasn't Come Yet, Baby," "He's Your Uncle, Not Your Dad," "Your Groovy Self," "There Ain't Nothing Like a Song."

Running time: 90 minutes
Release date: 6/13/68

Live
A Little,
Love
A Little

Metro-Goldwyn-Mayer

Michele Carey, Elvis Presley

Credits

Produced by Douglas Laurence.
Directed by Norman Taurog.
Screenplay by Michael A. Hoey
    and Dan Greenburg.
Based on the Novel *Kiss My Firm
And Pliant Lips* by Dan Greenburg.
Photographed by Fred Koenekamp,
    A.S.C.
Edited by John McSweeney, A.C.E.
Music Score by Billy Strange.
Art Direction by George Davis and
    Preston Ames.
Choreography by Jack Regas and
    Jack Baker.
Makeup by William Tuttle.
Assistant Director: Al Shenberg.
Technical Advisor: Colonel Tom
    Parker.
A Douglas Laurence Production.
Photographed in Panavision and
    Metrocolor.

Cast

Greg	Elvis Presley
Bernice	Michele Carey
Mike Landsdown	Don Porter
Penlow	Rudy Vallee
Harry	Dick Sargent
Milkman	Sterling Holloway
Ellen	Celeste Yarnall
Delivery Boy	Eddie Hodges
Robbie's Mother	Joan Shawlee
Miss Selfridge	Mary Grover
Receptionist	Emily Banks
Art Director	Michael Keller
1st Secretary	Merri Ashley
2nd Secretary	Phyllis Davis
Perfume Model	Ursula Menzel

Synopsis

Elvis is a young photographer who
has two jobs—one as a photographer
for a conservative publisher, Rudy
Vallee, and another as photographer
for girlie magazine publisher Don

Porter. There is a lot of running
around as Elvis tries to keep one
publisher from finding out about the
other. Michele Carey is a kooky
model who wants Elvis to enter into
a more adult relationship with her.

Songs

"Almost in Love," "A Little Less
Conversation," "Edge of Reality,"
"Wonderful World."

Running time: 89 minutes
Release date: 10/9/68

Elvis Presley, Don Porter

Michele Carey, Elvis Presley

Michele Carey, Sterling Holloway, Elvis Presley

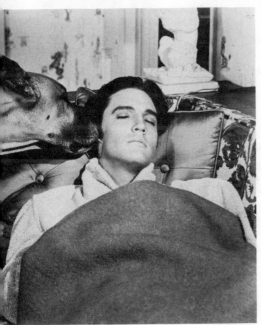

Charro

National General Pictures

Credits

Produced and Directed by Charles
   Marquis Warren.
Executive Producer: Harry A.
   Caplan.
Screenplay by Charles Marquis
   Warren.
Story by Frederic Louis Fox.
Photographed by Ellsworth
   Fredericks, A.S.C.
Edited by Al Clark, A.C.E.
Art Direction by James Sullivan.
Music Composed and Conducted by
   Hugo Montenegro.
Music Editor: John Mick.
Assistant Director: Dink Templeton.
Makeup by William Reynolds and
   Gene Bartlett.
Song, "Charro." Words and Music
   by Billy Strange and Scott Davis.
Technical Advisor: Colonel Tom
   Parker.
Photographed in Panavision and
   Technicolor.

Cast

Jesse Wade . . . . Elvis Presley
Tracey . . . . Ina Balin
Vince . . . . Victor French
Sara . . . . Barbara Werle
Billy Roy . . . . Solomon Sturges
Marcie . . . . Lynn Kellogg
Gunner . . . . James Sikking
Opie Keetch . . . . . . Paul Brinegar
Heff . . . . Harry Landers
Lt. Rivera . . . . Tony Young
Sheriff Ramsey . . . James Almanzar
Mody . . . . Charles H. Gray
Jerome Selby . . . . John Pickard
Martin Tilford . . . . . Garry Walberg
Gabe . . . . Duane Grey
Lige . . . . Rodd Redwing
Henry Carter . J. Edward McKinley

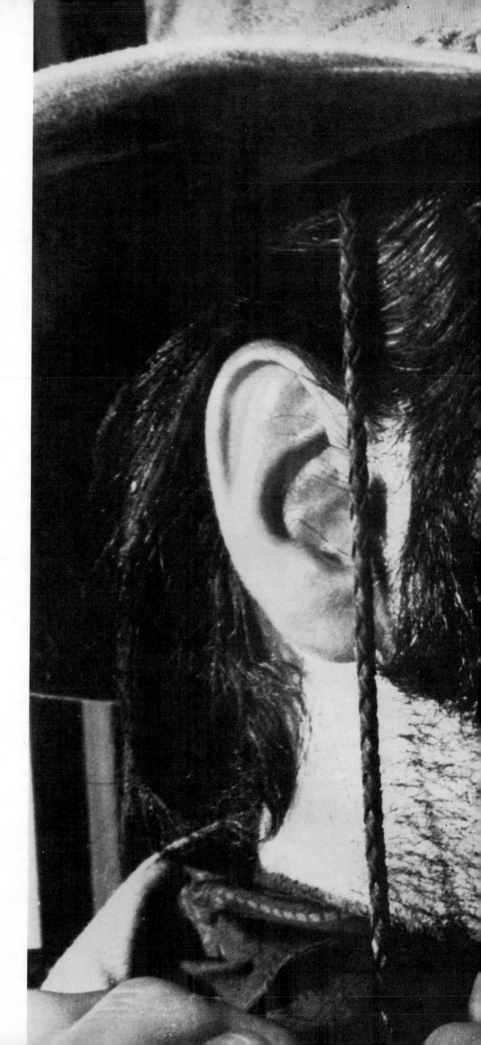

Synopsis

Elvis rides into a small Mexican town and is met by four gunmen, all members of the gang he once belonged to. Victor French, the leader, is sore at Elvis for leaving the gang and setting a bad example for the others. Victor decides to frame Elvis for the theft of a valuable gold and bronze victory cannon belonging to the Mexican government and worth $100,000.

The gang takes Elvis's horse and gun, leaving him for the Mexican Army to find and jail, while they take the cannon to the nearest safe town. Elvis captures a wild horse and rides after them.

When the sheriff, who is Elvis's friend, is shot by Victor's kid brother, Solomon Sturges, Elvis becomes sheriff and locks the kid in jail. Victor hears of this and hurries to town demanding the release of his kid brother or he'll start shooting up the town with his cannon.

The town is frightened and wants Elvis to release the killer, but Elvis refuses. When the cannon starts demolishing the town, building by building, Elvis takes the boy to the gang. There is a shoot-out and the cannon accidentally rolls over the boy, and Victor and his gang surrender to Elvis.

Elvis gathers up the cannon and the gang and heads for Mexico to clear his name and start living a new life with Ina Balin.

Songs

"Charro."

Running time: 98 minutes
Release date: 9/3/69

The Trouble With Girls

(and how to get into it)

Metro-Goldwyn-Mayer

Credits

Produced by Lester Welch.
Directed by Peter Tewksbury.
Screenplay by Arnold and
    Lois Peyser.
From the Novel by Day Keene and
    Dwight Babcock.
Based on a Story by Mouri Grashin.
Photographed by Jacques Marquette,
    A.S.C.
Edited by George W. Brooks.
Music Score by Billy Strange.
Art Direction by George W. Davis
    and Edward Carfagno.
Makeup by William Tuttle.
Technical Advisor: Colonel Tom
    Parker.
Photographed in Panavision and
    Metrocolor.

Marlyn Mason, Elvis Presley

Nicole Jaffe, Elvis Presley

Edward Andrews, Sheree North, Elvis Presley

Marlyn Mason, Edward Andrews, Elvis Presley

Elvis Presley, Marlyn Mason

the CHAUTAUQUA

Cast

Walter Hale .... Elvis Presley
Charlene .... Marlyn Mason
Betty .... Nicole Jaffe
Nita Nix .... Sheree North
Johnny .... Edward Andrews
Mr. Drewcolt ..... John Carradine
Caril .... Anissa Jones
Mr. Morality ...... Vincent Prince
Maude .... Joyce Van Polten
Willy .... Pepe Brown
Harrison Wilby .. Dabney Coleman
Mayor Gilchrist ...... Bill Zuchert
Mr. Perper .... Pitt Herbet
Clarence .... Anthony Teague
Constable .... Med Flory

Synopsis

Elvis is the manager of a Chautauqua, a rolling canvas college, moving from town to town spreading cultural knowledge. In one particular town Elvis gets into plenty of trouble with girls and a few assorted characters during a one-week stand. Trouble develops between the town locals and the Chautauqua personnel. There is the girl who wants to leave home to join the troupe. There is an illicit love affair that ends in murder. And a romance develops between Elvis and Marlyn Mason.

Songs

"Almost," "Clean Up Your Own Backyard."

Running time: 99 minutes
Release date: 12/10/69

Change of Habit

NBC-Universal

Credits
Produced by Joe Connelly.
Directed by William Graham.
Associate Producer: Irving Paley.
Screenplay by James Lee, S. S.
    Schweitzer and Eric Bercovici.
Based on a Story by John Joseph
    and Richard Morris.
Photographed by Russell Metty,
    A.S.C.
Edited by Douglas Stewart.
Music by William Goldenberg.
Technical Advisor: Colonel Tom
    Parker.
Color by Technicolor.

Cast
Dr. John Carpenter .. Elvis Presley
Sister Michelle · Mary Tyler Moore
Sister Irene ...... Barbara McNair
Sister Barbara .... Jane Elliot
Mother Joseph ...... Leorna Dana
Lt. Moretti .... Edward Asner
The Banker .... Robert Emhart
Father Gibbons .... Regis Toomey
Rose .... Doro Merande
Lily .... Ruth McDevitt
Bishop Finley .... Richard Carlson
Julio Hernandez.......Nefti Millet
Desiree .... Laura Figuerosa
Amanda .... Lorena Rich

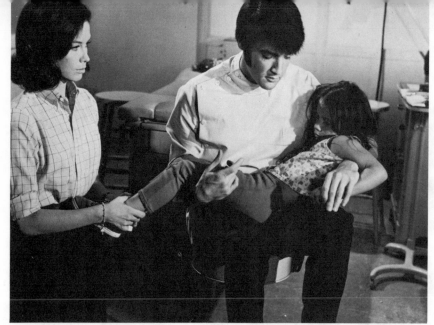

Mary Tyler Moore, Elvis Presley, Lorena Kirk

Jane Elliot, Elvis Presley

Mary Tyler Moore, Elvis Presley

Mary Tyler Moore, Elvis Presley, Lorena Kirk

Synopsis

Elvis is a hip, devoted doctor heading a clinic in a Latin-Negro slum neighborhood. Three nuns, Mary Tyler Moore, Barbara McNair and Jane Elliot, are instructed to do social work in the ghetto, and change their habit (nun's garb) in favor of modern dress. They do good work but their mission is misunderstood by more conservative elements in the Church and they must take up the habit again. Then Elvis discovers the nurse he loves is a nun.

After more good works, the girls are further misunderstood and sent back to the convent where Mary pines for Elvis. She returns to the old neighborhood to watch Elvis leading a rock 'n' roll mass. She must make a choice, Elvis or the Church. Which one she picks is left for the audience to decide.

Songs

"Change of Habit," Rubberneckin'," "Let Us Pray."

Running time: 93 minutes
Release date: 1/21/70

Lorena Kirk, Mary Tyler Moore, Elvis Presley

208

Elvis –
"That's the
Way It Is"
Metro-Goldwyn-Mayer

Credits
Directed by Denis Sanders.
Photographed by Lucien Ballard.
Edited by Henry Berman, A.C.E.
 and George Folsey, Jr.
Unit Production Manager: Dale
 Hutchinson.
Sound by Larry Hadsell and
 Lyle Burbridge.
Assistant Director: John Wilson.
Technical Advisor: Colonel Tom
 Parker.
Photographed in Panavision and
 Metrocolor.

Cast
Elvis Presley

Synopsis
A documentary on Elvis's act on
stage at the International Hotel in
Las Vegas and the days leading up
to the opening night.

Songs

"Mystery Train," "Tiger Man," "Words," "The Next Step Is Love," "Polk Salad Annie," "Crying Time," "Love Me," "That's All Right Mama," "Little Sister," "What'd I Say," "How the Web Was Woven," "Stranger in the Crowd," "I Just Can't Help Believing," "You Don't Have to Say You Love Me," "Bridge Over Troubled Waters," "You've Lost That Lovin' Feelin'," "Mary in the Morning," "I've Lost You," "Patch It Up," "Love Me Tender," "Sweet Caroline," "Heartbreak Hotel," "One Night with You," "Blue Suede Shoes," "All Shook Up," "Suspicious Minds," "Can't Help Falling in Love With You."

"Director Denis Sanders and cinematographer Lucien Ballard have created a very engaging picture. If you're an Elvis fan already, you'll love it. If you're not, you just might end up being one."
—Dawn A. Lospaluto
Newark Evening News

". . . Elvis is magnificent, more powerful than ever as he sings twenty-seven numbers, still one of the most compelling of all rock performers."
—Henry S. Resnik
Saturday Review

Running time: 107 minutes
Release date: 12/15/70

Elvis On Tour

Metro-Goldwyn-Mayer

Credits

Produced and Directed by
    Pierre Adidge and Robert Abel.
Associate Producer: Sidney Levin.
Photographed by Robert Thomas.
Technical Advisor: Colonel Tom
    Parker.
Color by Metrocolor.

Cast

Elvis Presley

Synopsis

A documentary about Elvis's national concert tour and "a tour of Elvis's life, a close-up of the birth and life of an American phenomenon."

Running time: 93 minutes
Release date: 6/6/73

The Elvis Presley Discography of Million Record Sellers

"Where words leave off, music begins."
—*Peter Ilyich Tchaikovsky*

The records listed here are only the million-plus sellers. They are all RCA or RCA Victor releases. This list is in no way a complete discography of Elvis's total record output. Jerry Hopkins' excellent biography *Elvis* offers a more comprehensive listing. The symbol GR means the Record Industry Association of America (RIAA) has presented Elvis a gold record. This certifies a million or more copies sold in the case of single records and EPs, one million dollars or more in retail sales for albums. Sometimes the claims made by RCA for a million-record seller and RIAA do not match.

SINGLES—78 rpm

Title	Release Date
Heartbreak Hotel	Jan., 1956
I Was the One	Jan., 1956
I Want You, I Need You, I Love You	May, 1956
Hound Dog	July, 1956
Don't Be Cruel	July, 1956
Love Me Tender	Sept., 1956
Any Way You Want Me	Sept., 1956
Too Much	Sept., 1956
Playing for Keeps	Sept., 1956
All Shook Up	Jan., 1957
That's When Your Heartbreak Begins	Jan., 1957
Teddy Bear	June, 1957
Loving You	June, 1957
Jailhouse Rock	Sept., 1957
Treat Me Nice	Sept., 1957
Don't	Dec., 1957
I Beg of You	Dec., 1957
Wear My Ring Around Your Neck	Apr., 1958
Hard Headed Woman	June, 1958 GR

SINGLES—45 rpm

Title	Release Date
I Got Stung	Oct., 1958
A Fool Such As I	Mar., 1959
A Big Hunk o' Love	June, 1959
Stuck on You	Mar., 1960
It's Now or Never	July, 1960
A Mess of Blues	July, 1960
Are You Lonesome Tonight	Nov., 1960
I Gotta Know	Nov., 1960
Surrender	Feb., 1961
I Feel So Bad	May, 1961
Little Sister	Aug., 1961
Can't Help Falling in Love	Nov., 1961 GR
Rock-a-Hula Baby	Nov., 1961
Good Luck Charm	Feb., 1962
Anything That's Part of You	Feb., 1962
She's Not You	July, 1962
Return to Sender	Oct., 1962
Where Do You Come From	Oct., 1962
One Broken Heart for Sale	Jan., 1963
(You're the) Devil in Disguise	June, 1963
Bossa Nova Baby	Oct., 1963
Kissin' Cousins	Oct., 1963
Viva Las Vegas	Apr., 1964
Ain't That Loving You	Sept., 1964
Crying in the Chapel	Apr., 1965
I'm Yours	Aug., 1965
Wooden Heart	Oct., 1965
If I Can Dream	Oct., 1968
In the Ghetto	Apr., 1969 GR
Suspicious Minds	Aug., 1969 GR
Don't Cry Daddy	Nov., 1969 GR
Kentucky Rain	Jan., 1970
The Wonder of You	May, 1970 GR

ALBUMS—45 rpm EP
ELVIS, VOL. 1, *1956 GR*
Rip It Up, Love Me, When My Blue Moon
Turns to Gold Again, Paralyzed

JAILHOUSE ROCK, *1957 GR*
Jailhouse Rock, Young and Beautiful,
I Want to Be Free, Don't Leave Me Now,
Baby, I Don't Care

ALBUMS—33 ⅓ rpm EP
ELVIS BY REQUEST:
FLAMING STAR, *Jan., 1961*
Flaming Star, Summer Kisses, Winter Tears,
Are You Lonesome Tonight, It's Now or Never

ALBUMS—33 ⅓ rpm LP
ELVIS PRESLEY, *Apr., 1956 GR*
Blue Suede Shoes, I'm Counting on You,
I Got a Woman, One-Sided Love Affair,
I Love You Because, Tutti Frutti, Trying to Get
to You, I'm Gonna Sit Right Down and Cry,
I'll Never Let You Go, Blue Moon, Money Honey

ELVIS, *Oct., 1957 GR*
Rip It Up, Love Me, When My Blue Moon Turns
to Gold Again, Long Tall Sally, First in Line,
Paralyzed, So Glad You're Mine, Old Shep,
Ready Teddy, Anyplace Is Paradise, How's the
World Treating You, How Do You Think I Feel

LOVING YOU, *July, 1957 GR*
Mean Woman Blues, Teddy Bear, Loving You,
Got a Lot of Lovin' to Do, Lonesome Cowboy,
Hot Dog, Party, Blueberry Hill, True Love,
Don't Leave Me Now, Have I Told You
Lately That I Love You, I Need You So

ELVIS'S CHRISTMAS ALBUM *Nov., 1957 GR*
Santa Claus Is Back in Town, White Christmas,
Here Comes Santa Claus, I'll Be Home for
Christmas, Blue Christmas, Santa Bring My
Baby Back, O Little Town of Bethlehem,
Silent Night, Peace in the Valley, I Believe, Take
My Hand, Precious Lord, It Is No Secret

ELVIS'S GOLDEN RECORDS, *Mar., 1958 GR*
Hound Dog, Loving You, All Shook Up,
Heartbreak Hotel, Jailhouse Rock, Love Me,
Too Much, Don't Be Cruel, That's When Your
Heartaches Begin, Teddy Bear, Love Me
Tender, Treat Me Nice, Any Way You Want Me,
I Want You, I Need You, I Love You

KING CREOLE, *Aug., 1958*
King Creole, As Long As I Have You, Hard
Headed Woman, Trouble, Dixieland Rock,
Don't Ask Me Why, Lover Doll, Crawfish,
Young Dreams, Steadfast, Loyal and True,
New Orleans

50,000,000 ELVIS FANS CAN'T BE WRONG
ELVIS'S GOLD RECORDS, VOL. 2
Dec., 1959 GR
A Fool Such As I, I Need Your Love Tonight,
Wear My Ring Around Your Neck, Doncha
Think It's Time, I Beg of You, A Big Hunk o'
Love, Don't, My Wish Came True, One Night,
I Got Stung

ELVIS IS BACK, *Apr., 1960*
Fever, Girl Next Door Went-a-Walking, Soldier
Boy, Make Me Know It, I Will Be Home Again,
Reconsider, Baby, It Feels So Right, Like a
Baby, The Girl of My Best Friend, Thrill of Your
Love, Such a Night, Dirty, Dirty Feeling

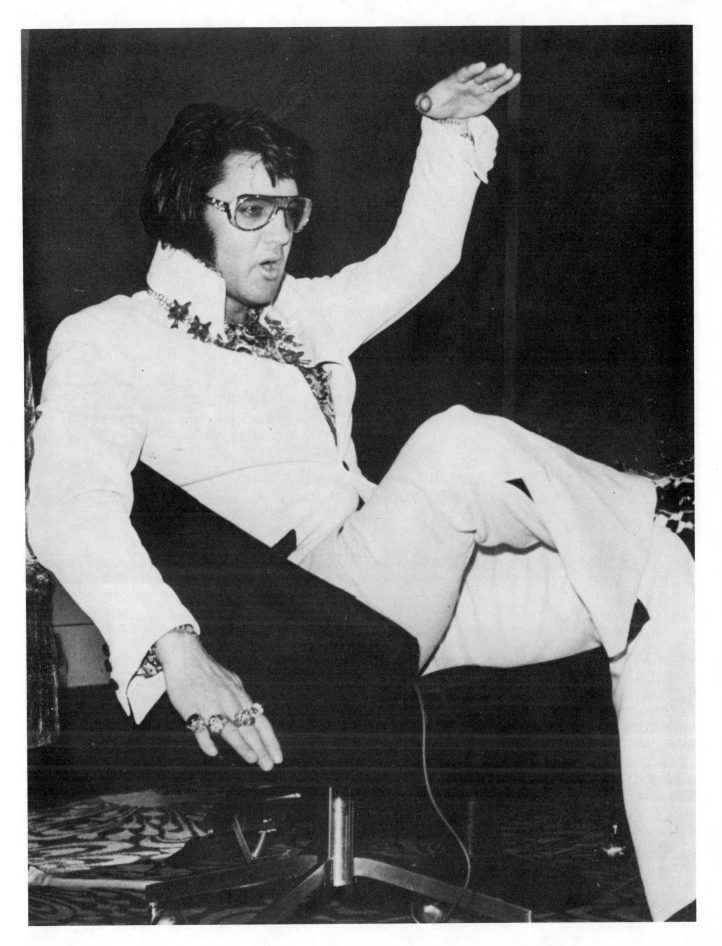

G.I. BLUES, *Oct., 1960 GR*
Tonight Is So Right For Love, What's She
Really Like, Frankfort Special, Wooden Heart,
G.I. Blues, Pocketful of Rainbows, Shoppin'
Around, Big Boots, Didja Ever, Blue Suede
Shoes, Doin' the Best I Can

HIS HAND IN MINE, *Dec., 1960 GR*
His Hand In Mine, I'm Gonna Walk Dem Golden
Stairs, In My Father's House, Milky White
Way, Known Only to Him, I Believe in the Man
in the Sky, Joshua Fit the Battle, Jesus Knows
What I Need, Swing Down, Sweet Chariot,
Mansion over the Hilltop, If We Never Meet
Again, Working on the Building

SOMETHING FOR EVERYBODY *June, 1961*
There's Always Me, Give Me the Right, It's a Sin,
Sentimental Me, Starting Today, Gently,
I'm Comin' Home, In Your Arms, Put the
Blame On Me, Judy, I Want You With Me,
I Slipped, I Stumbled, I Fell

BLUE HAWAII, *Oct., 1961 GR*
Blue Hawaii, Almost Always True, Aloha Oe,
No More, Can't Help Falling in Love,
Rock-a-Hula Baby, Moonlight Swim, Ku-u-i-po,
Ito Eats, Slicin' Sand, Hawaiian Sunset,
Beach Boy Blues, Island of Love, Hawaiian
Wedding Song

GIRLS! GIRLS! GIRLS!, *Nov., 1962 GR*
Girls! Girls! Girls!, I Don't Wanna Be Tied,
Where Do You Come From, I Don't Want To,
We'll Be Together, A Boy Like Me, A Girl
Like You, Earth Boy, Return to Sender, Because
of Love, Thanks to the Rolling Sea, Song of
the Shrimp, The Walls Have Ears, We're
Coming in Loaded

ELVIS'S GOLDEN RECORDS
VOL. 3, *Sept., 1963 GR*
It's Now or Never, Stuck on You, Fame and
Fortune, I Gotta Know, Surrender, I Feel So Bad,
Are You Lonesome Tonight, His Latest Flame,
Little Sister, Good Luck Charm, Anything
That's Part of You, She's Not You

FUN IN ACAPULCO, *Nov., 1963*
Fun in Acapulco, Vino, Dinero y Amor,
Mexico, El Toro, Marguerita, The Bullfighter
Was a Lady, No Room to Rhumba in a Sports
Car, I Think I'm Gonna Like It Here, Bossa
Nova Baby, You Can't Say No in Acapulco,
Guadalajara, Love Me Tonight, Slowly But Surely

ROUSTABOUT, *Oct., 1964*
Roustabout, Little Egypt, Poison Ivy League,
Hard Knocks, It's a Wonderful World, Big Love,
Big Heartache, One-Track Heart, It's Carnival
Time, Carny Town, There's a Brand New Day
on the Horizon, Wheels on My Heels

HOW GREAT THOU ART, *Mar., 1967 GR*
How Great Thou Art, In the Garden, Somebody
Bigger Than You and I, Farther Along, Stand
by Me, Without Him, So High, Where Could
I Go But to the Lord, By and By, If the Lord
Wasn't Walking By My Side, Run On, Where
No One Stands Alone, Crying in the Chapel

ELVIS (TV Special), *Dec., 1968 GR*
Trouble, Guitar Man, Lawdy, Miss Clawdy,
Baby, What You Want Me to Do, *Medley:*
(Heartbreak Hotel, Hound Dog, All Shook Up,
Can't Help Falling In Love, Jailhouse Rock),
Love Me Tender, Where Could I Go But to the
Lord, Up Above My Head, Saved, Blue
Christmas, One Night, Memories, *Medley:*
(Nothingville, Big Boss Man, Guitar Man, Little
Egypt, Trouble, If I Can Dream)

FROM ELVIS IN MEMPHIS, *May, 1969 GR*
Wearin' That Loved-on Look, Only the Strong

Survive, I'll Hold You in My Heart, Long
Black Limousine, It Keeps Right on A-Hurtin',
I'm Movin' On, Power of My Love, Gentle on
My Mind, After Loving You, True Love Travels
on a Gravel Road, Any Day Now, In the Ghetto

FROM MEMPHIS TO VEGAS/
FROM VEGAS TO MEMPHIS (two-record set)
Nov., 1969 GR
Blue Suede Shoes, Johnny B. Goode, All Shook
Up, Are You Lonesome Tonight, Hound Dog,
I Can't Stop Loving You, My Babe, Mystery
Train, Tiger Man, Words, In the Ghetto,
Suspicious Minds, Can't Help Falling in Love,
Inherit the Wind, This Is the Story, Stranger
in My Own Home Town, A Little Bit of Green,
And the Grass Won't Pay No Mind, Do You
Know Who I Am, From a Jack to a King,
The Fair's Moving On, You'll Think of Me,
Without Love